FROM NEW YORK TO SAN FRANCISCO

FROM NEW YORK
TO SAN FRANCISCO

Travel Sketches from the Year 1869

ERNST MENDELSSOHN-BARTHOLDY

Translated by BARBARA H. THIEM

Edited by GERTRUD GRAUBART CHAMPE

German edition by KARIN BÜRGER AND SEBASTIAN PANWITZ

INDIANA UNIVERSITY PRESS

This book is a publication of

Indiana University Press
Office of Scholarly Publishing
Herman B Wells Library 350
1320 East 10th Street
Bloomington, Indiana 47405 USA

iupress.indiana.edu

Library of Congress Cataloging-in-Publication Data

Names: Mendelssohn-Bartholdy, Ernst von, 1846–1909, author. | Champe, Gertrud
    Graubart, editor. | Burger, Karin, editor. | Panwitz, Sebastian, editor.
Title: From New York to San Francisco : travel sketches from the year 1869 / Ernst
    Mendelssohn-Bartholdy; translated by Barbara H. Thiem; edited by Gertrud Graubart
    Champe; German edition by Karin Burger and Sebastian Panwitz.
Other titles: Von New York nach San Francisco. English
Description: 1st edition. | Bloomington, Indiana : Indiana University Press, [2017] |
    Includes bibliographical references.
Identifiers: LCCN 2017025699 (print) | LCCN 2017019271 (ebook) | ISBN 9780253031228
    (ebook) | ISBN 9780253026316 (cloth : alk. paper)
Subjects: LCSH: United States—Description and travel. | Mendelssohn-Bartholdy,
    Ernst von, 1846–1909—Correspondence. | United States—Social life and customs—
    19th century. | Railroad travel—United States. | Travelers' writings, German.
Classification: LCC E168 (print) | LCC E168 .M53513 2017 (ebook) | DDC 917.304/
    09034—dc23
LC record available at https://lccn.loc.gov/2017025699

1 2 3 4 5   22 21 20 19 18 17

CONTENTS

TRANSLATOR'S NOTE

WHEN I CAME ACROSS the original private publication of these letters a few years ago, I was fascinated by the many aspects of American life in 1869 that are vividly reported. As one of the Mendelssohn family, I initially intended to translate this book for the many members of the clan who now live in this country and no longer speak German. However, I came to believe that these pages would be of interest to a larger public because they illustrate the vantage point of an educated European who spouts Latin quotations (for better or worse) and compares his experiences to his travels in Europe.

My thanks go to Gertrud Champe, who spent many hours making this translation idiomatic and flowing, and Jon Thiem, who helped us with his knowledge of the literature on the Mendelssohns and who was the first to discover the original book, as it was published privately in the nineteenth century.

Barbara H. Thiem

FROM NEW YORK TO SAN FRANCISCO

Introduction

LETTERS PROVIDE a rich and lively approach to cultural history; if the writing is sharply observant, they teach us a great deal about the time and place the writer is describing, no matter why the letters were written. Even as strangers, reading the letters long after they were written, we can let our imagination play among the cameos of the later-nineteenth-century United States that the present collection offers. The letters were composed in 1869, a time when the center of the country was moving westward after the end of the Civil War. In small settlements and large towns, people were building, for good and for ill, bringing with them elements of European civilization that ranged from newspapers to concerts of both European and American music, from city planning to the formation of communities based on faith. And for added divergence from what had been there, unalloyed for millennia, there was even a bit of authentic Chinese theater on the western shore.

The vast expanse of land was beginning to think of itself as one country. Financiers and industrialists had devoted imagination and funds to the construction of a continent-spanning railroad whose two arms, the Union Pacific and the Central Pacific, met and joined at Promontory, Utah, in May 1869. In many cities, black men and women were doing for pay what they had so recently done under duress. It was a time of ferment.

Into this bustling world came two privileged young Prussian men on holiday, Ernst Mendelssohn-Bartholdy and his older cousin Ernst

Westphal, both members of the Mendelssohn family of Berlin. Over a period of three months, they traveled across the United States and back again by train. During this time, no matter where they were, they sent word of their travels back home, enthusiastic about the sights and adventures they encountered and firmly convinced of their opinions about the way Americans conducted their affairs. Encountering their reports today provides a bittersweet opportunity to see ourselves as others saw us then.

All the letters in this collection are written by Ernst Mendelssohn-Bartholdy. Ernst Westphal is not necessarily a lesser personality, but as his cousin points out in one letter, he just doesn't like to write. His presence, however, must certainly have added to the pleasure and adventure of the excursion.

Mendelssohn-Bartholdy's early letters from New York are a colorful mixture of praise and criticism. Everything is exotic—the size, the noise, the banana he had for dessert, the beauty and freedom of the young women he sees (not that he enjoys the apparently subservient position into which these beauties put the men). And he is quick to praise the things he finds better in New York than in Berlin, like the general availability of streetcars, but he is quite ready to give the rough side of his tongue to whatever he finds distasteful, inappropriate, or even just unfamiliar.

Far from being an egalitarian, Ernst has an unfriendly or sarcastic word for any instance of people who think they are as good as anybody else. He pounces with a grin on a corrupt customs official:

> The customs officer who was inspecting my suitcase stood there comfortably, opening his hand behind his back saying: "You shan't have any trouble, Sir!" which I answered silently but pleasantly with a few dollars. The noble republican immediately signed my luggage with chalk, meaning that the bags were properly "fixed."

Nor does Ernst spare his cousin a few gibes when he refuses to use the same expedient to shorten their time of dealing with authority. Westphal, servant of the law, will not resort to bribery.

But for all his sniping at servants who don't serve, at riffraff with no manners, at the "exaggerated elegance" of women's clothes, Ernst has a certain sensitivity for the allure of New York, which was already a great world city:

I still feel strange when I write New York at the head of my letters and notice with every step on the street or even from my room into the corridor of the hotel that I am far, far away. New York is an overwhelming place. Even though there is nothing to see here, it is hard to describe what all one *can* see. There are no galleries, no museums,* no palaces. But the customs, the street life, the position and layout of the city would take more time to study properly and in depth than Dresden with its gallery, Venice with the Academy or other cities where art products fascinate our interest in the same way that material products do here.

About some things, however, Ernst is quite tone deaf, even according to the beliefs and sensitivities of his own time. He relates that many races are represented here:

> We see large numbers of black, brown, red-brown people, mulattos and mestizos. Half the coachmen, especially the private vehicle drivers, are Colored, many of the servants, maids, nurses and workmen also. Ernst and I are planning to buy a little pickaninny and bring him to Europe as our servant. Don't be surprised if you see us appear in such company!

Ernst became more informed and more nuanced about questions of racial interaction and the differences between North and South, thanks to detailed explanations he received from a Virginia gentleman, later on in his travels. This increase of information that we often think of as the reward of travel had many chances of occurring, thanks to the great variety of people the young men encountered, either through letters of introduction or through the luck of travel. The new acquaintances were forthcoming with information and generous with hospitality. Among the many friends the travelers made were some who were not born Yankees but Germans who had come to America in the revolutionary days of 1848 and established themselves securely in the professions or politics. People like this were very friendly to the two men and in several towns and cities, including New York, provided the underpinnings of their social life.

The two travelers could have had a splendid time in New York alone, but their program was to travel, and they began by heading to Boston, to attend a mammoth Peace Festival with parades, choruses of thousands, and, to Ernst's delight, music by his uncle, Felix Mendelssohn. The high

---

* The Metropolitan Museum of Art opened its doors on February 20, 1872.

point was an appearance by the president of the United States. Shortly after seeing the president from afar, the two men traveled to Washington, D.C., and on the strength of the letters of introduction they carried with them, they managed to have a friendly ten-minute interview with President Grant. For once, Ernst admitted that he was thrilled.

The train that would take them to Boston was quite different from a European one; to pass through New York, the train was disassembled, and then each car was drawn by horses from 24th Street to 42nd Street, where the train was reassembled and sent on its way. Of great and gory interest to the two Berliners as they watched these proceedings was the cowcatcher, the likes of which they had never seen. Railroading—the differences between American and European trains; the occasional sketchiness of rail line construction, compared to the luxury of first-class accommodations over some stretches; and the opportunities for drama when traveling on this just-completed cross-continental railroad—is one of the strong centers of interest of Ernst's account.

The letters have sometimes been described as a series of picture postcards, the same things that any tourist would tick off a list. But that is really not the point; in many cases, it is what they saw along the way, between the beauty points, that attracts interest today. With very little artifice, Ernst gives impressions of a country in the making: "What caught my attention is that everything seems finished only far enough to hold together or be serviceable. Streets are only partly or incompetently paved, some are still dirty and swampy, others partly sandy...." He writes about the creation of cities, about whole houses being moved from one lot to another as towns configure themselves, about the enthusiastic industry of people digging undreamed-of riches out of the earth in the far West, and, unforgettably, about Mormons creating their own world in the desert.

The account of social dynamics does not overwhelm the narrative of the American journey. The natural wonders, the tourist scenes the men visited—Mammoth Caves, Niagara Falls, the Mississippi River, the sight of Salt Lake in the distance, the "Big Trees" of California—did not fail to impress, and in the hands of the man who wrote home about them, they were described with some sensitivity. These chaps, who in the towns seemed to resist being impressed by what they saw, had no choice but to stand in awe of the power and beauty of America's geography. But instead

of really admitting it, they made a manly joke of their amazement by sending home a picture of themselves from California looking like a couple of
sun-bleached gold diggers.

The cousins had not been sure, originally, whether they should forge
westward as far as California, given the possibilities of disaster on the
newly completed railroad or at the hands of Indians, whom they had been
advised to fear. However, when they made their final inquiries in St. Louis
as to whether they should go, the answer was a rousing, unanimous "Yes."
In announcing their decision to his parents, Ernst wrote:

> The main reason we wish to head further and further west is that America
> is stranger and more remarkable the further we travel from eastern parts.
> Watching culture as it moves forward from the east, step by step, sending
> out the pioneers of civilization westward—that can really be called an
> adventure.

And yet Ernst sets out on his adventure in a rather inflexible state of
mind. He already believes he knows what any "educated person" would
hope for or want in his life. He admits that spending any long stretch of
time in any of the American cities of the West would be "quite horrible
and practically impossible" for him and that this is due in part to the "republican constitution to which I have more aversion the more I experience
its effects. I already had this tendency from reading and here, I mistrust
the communist tendencies which are of course more evident in a republic
than in a monarchy." In describing the westward adventure, Ernst creates a set piece, an exposition of the royalist convictions at which he hints
throughout his letters. From these lines, it seems unlikely that, whatever
new information or experiences he may encounter, he will ever change
the convictions that allow him to say, "I can tolerate the political equality
of all classes, but flirting with social equality is insupportable, since only
dreamers can believe in it." But once arrived in San Francisco, the cousins
interrupted their exploration of the city to explore the hinterlands. In spite
of complaints about heat, dirt, and primitive accommodations, this may
have been the most pleasurable portion of their trip. There is not so much
sociological observation and more homage to nature.

After California, the road led back east. Not so many details are re-
corded for this leg of the trip. Chicago is reported with much praise,

and Ernst, a businessman in the making, realized the city's potential for commercial greatness. There follows a report on stops in Toronto and Montreal. Finally, drawing near the end of their journey, they come to Saratoga, the great spa and society meeting place of the time. Ending his account as he began, Ernst unleashes a diatribe against the lack of taste, the senseless exaggeration, and the excesses of women's dress. He bemoans the vulgarity of new money compared to the restraint of European old money and ends with a last little jab at President Grant, "his American Majesty." With a final stay in New York, an Atlantic crossing, and two weeks in Paris, the adventure ends with a stouthearted "Hurrah for the Old Country!" in English.

What has the intrepid adventurer, young Ernst Mendelssohn-Bartholdy, left us to see about ourselves? He described both the grandeur of nature and the silly grandiloquence of a young nation on the go, but not the high culture and high society of New England, which he noticed but had no time to observe in detail. He noticed but was not able to come to grips with the dynamics of the Civil War and what its consequences were going to be, nor with the interaction between the postwar North and South. He showed us the hustle of a new country coming together, with an apparently insatiable greed for money to be made, restless expansion, and a great eagerness for things that are the biggest and the longest and generally the most grandiose in the world. But he also showed us the soaring imagination that builds cities and the American generosity and bravery that are much to be admired and greatly to be prized. All these things are still there today, and can be recognized, willy-nilly, with a little push from Ernst. Riding cross-country on the train today, one can see it all: the mistakes that come from greed, attempts at achieving the biggest and the best, endless expanses of parking lots, highways, railyards, and cause for human tears . . . But one can also see the amber waves of grain, the purple mountains, the alabaster cities . . .

* * *

After reading to the end of a memoir, one is tempted to wonder what happened next, what became of the narrator. In our story, the answer is clear. On his return home, Ernst slipped back into the role to which he was born, as though his splendid trip had never been.

Ernst Mendelssohn-Bartholdy was born in Berlin on December 13, 1846, to the family founded by the philosopher and silk merchant Moses Mendelssohn (1729–1786), a definitive voice in the Jewish enlightenment of the eighteenth century. The source of the family's wealth was in the textile industry, and later, in banking. Ernst's father, Paul Mendelssohn-Bartholdy (1812–1874), was a grandson of Moses, brother of the composer-siblings Fanny Hensel and Felix Mendelssohn Bartholdy, and a partner in the banking house of Mendelssohn & Co. His mother, Albertine (1814–1879), was the daughter of the banker Heinrich Carl Heine and Henriette Mertens. Active in the business and intellectual life of Prussia, both parents had converted from Judaism to Protestantism, a fairly widespread phenomenon among educated secular Jews of the time. It is clear from remarks in Ernst's letters that by the time of his birth, the family was prosperous and securely seated at the higher levels of Berlin's civic life.

Ernst completed his secondary education in the winter of 1863–64 and spent the next year attending university lectures. After this, in accordance with his plan to enter the family's banking house, he embarked on a course of business study. By the spring of 1869, the young man had completed his training, but before beginning to build his career, he set out with his cousin, Ernst Westphal, and the support of his family, to travel to America and cross the continent by train. The letters in this book are a record of the trip, some reflections on the early capitalism of post-Civil War America, and an intimation of what his life and opinions would be after he returned home.

Ernst's father would probably not have treated his son to an extensive and expensive trip across America only because he doted on him; he would have wanted to gain some observations relevant to the family's business interests. And indeed, the Mendelssohn Bank was apparently interested to know whether it would be advantageous to invest in the new American railroad network.

In the course of their travels, Mendelssohn-Bartholdy and Westphal had ample opportunity to become acquainted with the structure, function, and reliability of the American railroad system, since with few exceptions, their entire journey was made by train. From personal experience, Ernst Mendelssohn-Bartholdy describes the different kinds of cars and classes, the technical innovations, and the peculiarities of the personnel.

Traveling from the East Coast to the West Coast by train had been possible for only a few months at this point. After the end of the Civil War in 1865, work had started on the transcontinental connection between the Pacific and the more densely populated areas east of the Rocky Mountains. The work was completed on May 10, 1869, when the two stretches—the Union Pacific Railroad and the Central Pacific Railroad—were connected at Promontory Summit near Salt Lake City, Utah. Only two months later, in July, our two travelers passed this point.

Apparently Ernst's jolly account in the letters did not completely reflect his thoughts about the American railroad system. Shortly after his return to Berlin, in November 1869, he wrote to his cousin, Karl Mendelssohn Bartholdy:

> I would like to counsel you right away, as an answer to your question in this regard, to dismiss any thought of investing in the American railroad system. Unfortunately, I can't at present send you a newspaper article about the Pacific Railroad line because all those sent to me by the editors have already been requisitioned by the numerous family members here. But I will try to obtain one and send it to you. Once you have read the article, I won't have to dissuade you further from being interested in the American railroads. The investors who got caught in the trap were taken advantage of in the worst way by the directors of the company; administration and supervision are pitiable; in short: *noli tangere*. What I say about these is true of almost all the railroads in the United States, some more, some less so.

In the event, Mendelssohn & Co.'s foreign investments were not made in the United States but continued to be made in the Russian Empire, with an emphasis on railroads. This commercial orientation proved to be a successful strategy and as Ernst's seniority in the bank grew, his cultivation of Russia as an investment partner contributed to the significant rise of Mendelssohn & Co, which became one of the wealthiest German private banks.

Ernst joined the bank in the fall of 1869, on his return from America, and rose steadily in office and influence. By 1871 he was a partner, and from January 1, 1875, he was co-head of the banking house, together with his cousin, Franz Mendelssohn. In 1889, on the death of Franz, Ernst Mendelssohn-Bartholdy became senior head of the bank at age forty-

three. His leadership of the family's banking house was highly successful, bringing growth and honor to the company. Ernst was also active in
domestic politics outside the bank itself, and internationally, supporting
German colonialism in Africa and other policies of Emperor William
II. His collaboration with the work of the Prussian chancellor, Otto von
Bismarck, was highly visible and as open-handed as only the dispositions
of an indescribably rich and ambitious man could make it. On two different occasions, he provided large sums of money that allowed Bismarck to
carry out programs that might otherwise not have been possible. His ac-
tions and his competence did not go unnoticed; in 1892, the great banker
was invited to take part in the reform of the Stock Market Law.

Toward the end of the nineteenth century, one branch of the Mendelssohn family had been raised into the Prussian hereditary aristocracy. The
honor was accepted quietly, and the family continued to live in the solid
but unpretentious way that had characterized it for generations. This was
not entirely the case with Ernst, of whom it was said that up to his day, no
Mendelssohn had sought political influence so openly, accumulated such
riches, or designed for himself such an ostentatious lifestyle. In attempting
to get a sense of Ernst's life, one must balance this way of living against
what is known about Ernst's strong sense of duty and responsibility to the
family, the bank, and the German Prussian state. And yet one remembers
what he had to say about American conspicuous consumption.

Ernst's embrace of visibility may have had some relation to his desire
to be ennobled himself, but it was not sufficient that he worked to expand
the reach of Mendelssohn & Co., took active part in domestic and foreign
politics, cultivated his connections with people in high places, and made
more than generous contributions to civic projects. He was blocked by
society's deep-seated anti-Semitism, and a patent of nobility was slow in
coming. As a reason for the denial, Emperor William's advisers cautioned
that ennoblement as a reward for these contributions to the Prussian economy, and later to the imperial economy, would help create a "stock market
nobility" and dilute the stern Prussian ethos.

In 1892, Ernst took a step that may have expressed more appropriately
his desire to be part of the stuff and fabric that made his country noble and
strong. From a member of his own social circle, Ernst bought an ancient
estate, east of Berlin in the territory of the Junker caste, the landed nobility

who in many respects were the true leaders of Germany from the late nine-teenth through the early twentieth century. The influence and policies of these powerful men, leaders in military, political, and agricultural affairs, permeated the entire country, under the leadership of chancellor Otto von Bismarck, himself a Junker.

By 1895, Ernst Mendelssohn-Bartholdy had prepared his case. His for-mal address to Emperor William II listed his professional achievements as a contribution to the nation, worthy to be rewarded by the granting of a title of hereditary nobility. The first response to this application, from Wil-liam's adviser in the Department of Heraldry, the previously mentioned polite but clearly anti-Semitic negative, was based on the doctrine of *Blut und Boden* (Blood and Soil) developed and applied in late nineteenth-century Germany. Those who espoused these two criteria for being a true German maintained that Jewish blood would dilute the virtuous strain that made Germany great. But with the emperor's assent, this negative opinion against Ernst was countermanded by the Minister of the Imperial Household, and Ernst became Ernst von Mendelssohn-Bartholdy.

This is the status of Ernst von Mendelssohn-Bartholdy at the culmina-tion of his career: he is the intermediary between the German and the Russian governments in matters of economic policy; a member of the Prussian House of Lords; a well-known philanthropist; and bearer of many titles, the greatest of which is "true Privy Councilor with the title Excellency." In 1909, the year of his death, Ernst was the richest inhabitant of the city of Berlin, second only to the emperor.

Throughout his life, Ernst had had the opportunity to experience ease and status, participate in the growth and development of a remarkable family, exercise his intelligence in the creation of public policy, wield power, and contribute to the honor and welfare of Prussia and the Ger-man Empire. Moreover, although he and his family and untold others had to observe and endure the wounds of anti-Semitic discrimination, it was not his lot to see the destruction of resolutely German Mendelssohn lives and fortunes that came later. We see him in a late portrait, conscious that he has run a good race, erect, dignified, and perhaps with a slight smile.

This story of a grand German family ranging far from home does not fade away with Ernst Mendelssohn-Bartholdy and his cousin Ernst West-phal. An echo of the young Prussian adventurers who made the great

American train trip of 1869 still sounds in the twenty-first century, and the last word is related, however distantly, to quiet Ernst Westphal. His great-niece, Helene, a sixth-generation descendant of the family of Moses Mendelssohn, in some sense completed a circular path begun in the eighteenth century when the family started participating in the founding and shaping of Prussia's civic and commercial life. It would be fascinating to hear her articulate the considerations and beliefs that brought this daughter of assimilated, upper-class German Jews back to giving full and active expression, in perilous times, to her Jewish origins and heritage.

The *Encyclopedia* of the Jewish Women's Archive presents Helene Westphal, later known as Leni Yahil, as a committed activist in the Jewish youth movement in pre–World War II Germany, a willing worker in Palestine, and a prolific scholar in Israel. Before being forced to leave Germany, Yahil was a student at the College of Judaic Studies in Berlin. A leader of the Jewish youth movement, she migrated to Palestine in 1934, where she both worked and studied. She earned a PhD from the Hebrew University in Jerusalem, conferred in 1965, with a doctoral dissertation titled "The Jews of Denmark during the Holocaust." In 1942, she married Chaim Yahil, who became an Israeli diplomat. As Leni Yahil, she was an eminent Holocaust historian and teacher. Her chef d'oeuvre is *The Holocaust: The Fate of European Jewry (1932–1945)*, published in English in 1990.

Leni Yahil lived until 2007. She chose to live and act and work as a Jew, with the same excellence as that exhibited by her ancestors who chose to become assimilated. Looking at her work and Ernst's, her travels and his side by side, demonstrates two different responses by a great family to the same ancient challenge thrown down at different times and places. The contrast is enlivened by Ernst's stimulating and entertaining letters. They have been carefully translated here by a Mendelssohn descendant of the eighth generation, to be available for further research and for enjoyable reading.

Gertrud Graubart Champe

Ernst (von) Mendelssohn-Bartholdy, 1870. © Bernhard Thévoz

Ernst Westphal. © Sebastian Panwitz

The Letters

Hurray for the Old Country!

On Board the *Scotia*[1]

Saturday June 5, 1869

Dearest parents!

I can't wait to chat with you from dry land, so I am beginning this letter if not on swaying feet, at least on the swaying seats of our Atlantic vessel and will finish it in New York.

Let me start this first sign of life from the New World with heartfelt greetings.

As I write, it has been six days since I left solid ground and I am likely three days away from stepping on it again. Directly to the north of us is the pole, to the south the equator; the closest distance to land is 900 miles. It is a strange idea for this landlubber to write a letter under such circumstances, though not stranger than my being in a situation like this to start with. The long companionship with the ocean as well as with the ship, the life on board, and the fellow travelers are all new and unusual indeed. Everything is as strange, unique, and interesting as I pictured it when you and I, dear mother, were looking at an American steamer in Hamburg a year ago and trying to imagine the cabins, reception rooms, and life on board as I am experiencing it now. When I earnestly wished that I could take a trip on such a ship, you answered, almost laughing, "Why don't you?" At that time, we both believed this was impossible. Whenever I consider in how short a time this impossibility was realized I am tempted to jump for joy!

Now for the facts and statistics—those you have more right to expect from me than old memories. Let me describe our trip so far.

We (my cousin and traveling companion Ernst Westphal and I. We left from Queenstown at Ireland's southern coast) left the coast, as I reported in my last letter, at 11 a.m. last Sunday in a tender, crossing the imposing harbor for about 30 minutes (it is supposedly the second most important for England's navy), till we reached the *Scotia* anchored at the mouth of the harbor. The passengers who had been on board since Liverpool inspected us newcomers climbing the stairs from the deck with as much curiosity as is natural after a trip of 18 hours on the open ocean with nothing but water in sight. Having passed through this crossfire from above we caught sight of the all-powerful captain[2] who had planted himself with his first officers precisely across from the spot where we alighted. His snow white hair, fat belly, and important mien were all specially adopted to impress his shy future subjects. This old sea hero is not the most pleasant of men; he would rather show his sense of absolute power. His officers naturally imitate him and are distant and inaccessible.

I might as well mention our fellow travelers in the same context: precious few of them deserve a different opinion, though for different reasons. Most of them are Americans, native Yankees, with bad manners and little education; a few German-Americans, i.e. more recent immigrants, are especially bad; only one person deserves our interest: the old philanthropist Peabody, famous for his charity, having only recently given a million pounds sterling to the poor. But even he disturbs us if through no fault of his own; he suffers from a terrible cough which reminds us of his presence all too often since his cabin is right next to ours. Among the ladies there are a few adorable girls whom I tried to approach in the beginning; however, they soon almost all came down with seasickness and are now invisible. There is a rather pleasant Spaniard with whom I chat frequently. At the risk of being unjust to some of the other passengers I can't change my general opinion: I have found so many of the previously mentioned type that I can't be reproached for having stopped trying to make new discoveries. Ernst and I are reserved, answer when approached, but otherwise do not exert ourselves.

One engaging thing is the language of those German-Americans, mostly from Pennsylvania, whose dialect is proverbial and infamous even in America. One of them addresses everyone informally and, for example, tells me the following nonsense: *"Siescht Du, dasch noisechen of die Niagara-Falls ist something ganz enormous."* Isn't that too much? Had Ernst and I not both heard this sentence we would not have believed it. *Noisechen* is supposed to be "small noise" and no doubt a joke!

However, I have skipped some of my history, have not even mentioned that after we passed the captain the steward led us to our cabin, where we installed ourselves comfortably. As expected, its location is excellent and fulfills all our wishes with the possible exception of a screaming infant (who was moved by the second night on the strength of my repeated complaints to the purser, who himself is no husband and whose nerves, like mine, are not inured to such musical sounds) and "Uncle" Peabody as we call him. As for the furnishings of the small private cabins called "staterooms," you have seen them. For the rest I refer to the first chapter of Dickens' *American Notes*[3] where they are aptly described. Just like his, our disappointment was almost comical as we took in the reality of our tight staterooms as contrasted with the almost fairy tale image put forth by the travel agent in London.

The mail was not expected before 4 o'clock so we had time to arrange our things without staggering and to get the lay of the ship, which is no small matter on this enormous vessel. On this trip it is not completely full. The number of passengers does not top 180 in first class and about 20 in second. There are no between-deck passengers; the *Scotia* as well as other ships of the Cunard Line does not have this custom. No doubt that is the reason why this company is preferred to the lines from Bremen or Hamburg, which all sell between-deck places. Ships with emigrants, especially when full, are better avoided because of infectious diseases and epidemics, quite apart from the danger of chaos in an emergency when there are more passengers.

All the rooms on the *Scotia* are elegant. The ladies have a large drawing room to themselves; two others, one in front and the other in the rear of the ship, are for "all the world" (which does not mean that I would call the first mentioned half the world). The navigator cabin only projects from the deck far enough so that the heads of the navigators are visible; they receive their orders through a pneumatic tube system from the bridge between the paddle boxes and from other points of the ship where officers are stationed. During the day, the captain tends to stay in a small house which he had built on deck and which looks like a miniature summer villa. It is supported by strong iron stakes and will not easily be swept away by a storm. This enclosure is erected at a point where the ship sways least, which makes me believe the rumor among the passengers that our captain tends to get sick at the beginning of each trip.

Around 4 o'clock, we gradually started moving. We watched the little mail steamer leave the coast and follow us out onto the ocean, catching up so we would not lose more time. It reached us in about 45 minutes. An endless number of mail bags with European correspondence were heaved over. As soon as that was done, the pilot guide jumped onto the little steamer. By his leaving us, the last connection with Europe was severed. The next land we would see would be America—or nothing. Just as I was thinking about that and watching the steamer increase its distance, the steward brought me a telegram. My first thought was: Could I still return? My second thought and a look at the boat that was close but not close enough showed me the impossibility of such a course of action. You can imagine with what great anxiety I now opened the telegram. And then it turned out to be a last greeting from a friend in London! The first telegram I ever opened with a beating heart; my pleasure at his attentiveness was slightly spoilt. But since this had turned out not to be a problem, our anxiety, Ernst's and mine, passed soon enough; it was swallowed up with lunch, which had been served in the dining hall by now.

Since we had reserved last, we unfortunately had our seats assigned close to the end of the hall where the movement of the vessel is the strongest. So far, there was no disadvantage because the ship moved calmly till late evening, when we went to bed. The entire time the Irish coast still accompanied us. We passed several lighthouses and communicated with another ship by rocket. Only when it turned completely dark did I go down to the cabin. It had been getting rather cold on deck so a group of men and I found a place near the smokestack, which was tolerably comfortable. The captain did us the honor of joining us there and proceeded to explain the difference between screw and paddle steamers and their relative advantages.

I slept quite well, but when I got up the next morning everything had changed as if by magic. The ship danced merrily on the long waves of the ocean, which by now was unbounded by a coastline in any direction: the sky was overcast and it was so cold that a winter suit, overcoat, and thick blanket did not protect sufficiently. Breakfast is scheduled for 8:30, lunch at 12:00, dinner at 4:00, and tea at 8:00. I proceeded to the first but was not comfortable in the closed room, thought the portions and teacups far too big (that's a good sign, don't you think?), and hurried back to the deck, where I took up station near the paddle boxes as the calmest place, right next to the "summer villa," and like a good soldier on duty did not leave the place all day. It felt strange: as long as I sat there I had no sign of discomfort except from the cold and wind. But as soon as I walked up and down or wanted to enter a drawing room, my stomach counseled me decidedly against it. And so I sat, not a corpse but quite immobile. My steward brought me lunch, dinner, and tea on deck. I ate it all with good appetite and felt decidedly good. When evening came I ran down to the cabin, ripped my clothes off as fast as I could, jumped into bed, felt completely safe again, and slept well. The next morning the movement of the boat had, if anything, increased. I got dressed like lightning (getting dressed or undressed were the most dangerous moments), ran to my old place on deck, ate, drank, and sat there again till evening, when I went to bed quickly as on the day before. This worked as a kind of radical cure against seasickness; the rough air and cold beat upon my face so harshly that the skin was already peeling on the first day and I still look incredibly ugly today. It is no small thing to sit outside in those temperatures for 13 hours without interruption, in the kind of wind that sprays the soup off your spoon as you try to eat it, something I experienced to my disadvantage when I tried a cup of strong beef tea for the first time. But my stubbornness was rewarded: I have not been seasick and would guess that it won't happen anymore now.

The dining hall looked quite different on the second day from the first, when everyone was merry and boisterous and none left their seats unoccupied. Anyone who has been to sea for a time must have had such experiences. Ernst, who has been a regular in the dining hall and has been completely immune to seasickness as well as any discomfort, reports that there were more benches than people. Many, even most of the passengers, have not surfaced again. Last Wednesday, the sun came out even though the cold did not diminish. The sea became calmer and some of the corpses came up on deck with pitiful faces. I had by then become quite lively and used to the motion, and walked around like someone who had never sat still, looking at the miserable ones with deep contempt—the most telling sign of how close I had been to the same state. This day of calm was advantageous because the next Thursday brought more hardship to many. When I looked at my barometer around noon I found it changed by half an inch. At a temperature of 5 degrees,[4] strong rain started, together with gusty winds that roiled up the ocean in no time. It lasted all night till this morning, when the sun is trying to appear again, none too soon for our ailing comrades.

Monday June 7
The weather has been splendid since the day before yesterday, though the ocean is hardly smooth as a mirror and the ship keeps rocking. But any suspicion of seasickness is past and I enjoy seeing the wind fill our sails, which we use as often as practical. We witnessed a spectacle which can be viewed more calmly on big ships than on smaller ones: fog enveloped us so that we could not see thirty steps ahead. This lasted from Friday evening till Sunday noon with brief interruptions, a tense situation for passengers and crew alike. Two sailors and an officer stood rigidly at the bow, staring into the fog, ready to give the alarm as soon as they sighted another ship; on the bridge three men kept a lookout and the big steam whistle sounded at short intervals to warn any ships close by. This sound was especially eerie during the night. All of us heaved a sigh of relief yesterday after lunch when we realized that the fog was gone. The apprehensive mood of the passengers disappeared magically. We appreciated the expanse of the ocean, the blue of the sky, and the glow of the sun twice as much as before. Even the animals seemed to like the change: masses of little whales called grampus played around the ship, their water fountains spewing all around.

I should mention also that we had a solemn church service in the drawing room yesterday morning. Sitting behind a pulpitlike desk, the captain read the liturgy according to the Anglican Church and after that, a sermon; any sailors and officers who were not on duty listened in their Sunday best; they had Bibles and hymn books, which were also shared with the passengers. We sang in a rather festive atmosphere. Such a mood seems natural on the ocean where people are so completely cut off.

Yesterday for the first time we saw another ship on the horizon. Just imagine: for the first time in seven days! We are advancing fast. To the joy of our crew, we have just passed a second ship, which turned out to be full of emigrants. We are in hourly expectation of the pilot. The captain predicts we may reach the coast and New York this evening still.

Monday evening

Punctually at 1:00, a pilot came on board. We were still 300 miles away from the mainland. He came in a schooner, having been on his way since June 1. So news and newspapers were not of recent date, but were received eagerly nevertheless. We will reach the harbor tonight. I regret that because we will not get to see the approach into New York harbor, supposedly one of the most beautiful in the world. We will stay on board till tomorrow morning. You may imagine how curious I am about what will happen next. I am too restless to continue writing and will proceed downstairs to pack my belongings, far too early, of course.

5ᵗʰ Avenue Hotel
New York, Tuesday June 8

It is the evening of our arrival day. Even though I left the ship at 7:00 this morning, I have only just now had a chance to sit down. The day was restlessly busy, maybe especially when compared to the previous seven days of complete idleness.

It is a refreshing thought that we have managed our entry onto solid ground. This entry was quite unpleasant. In the customs house where we were sent directly from the ship, we were tortured unreasonably, thanks to our friends who had sent with us a number of presents for relatives over here. We should take this to heart and not send things with traveling friends in order to save postal or customs expenses. The fact that you received the telegram of our happy landing half a day later than intended is thanks to a pretty silk dress. I can't deny that this makes me quite angry and has spoilt the joy of arrival considerably. We had to wait for two hours at customs till the agent arrived and collected the customs payment ($4). I was waiting on tenterhooks because I had planned to pass by the telegraph office to send you a confirmation before proceeding to the hotel. Now this silly situation arose. But that was not all: other passengers had taken all the carts so that we lost a lot of time trying to find another one. In short I only managed to send a telegram at 4:00, something that could easily have been done 8 hours earlier without this annoying circumstance. I will purchase a scalping knife and use it on the sinners when I get back.

So now I have cursed enough and can enjoy with you, as my telegram implies, that our trip here has turned out so well. I am sitting in the biggest and most beautiful of New York's hotels and have just shared a bottle of California wine with Ernst, toasting your health. I had bananas for dessert.

I am writing this letter in a big open hall which is terribly drafty and noisy: more than 100 people are chattering. Others are sitting in easy chairs and reading newspapers from Louisiana and San Francisco, while their hats are in the strangest positions and their legs are pushed against the wall at some height, "Black Brothers" are standing around, etc., etc. In this foreign-seeming place there is a definite southern flavor, which is natural since New York is on the same latitude as Rome and Naples.

The weather is pleasant, but quite warm. Around noon, there was a wild thunderstorm. I can't report on the city since I have not seen much of it yet; that will follow in the next few days. I will only mention that I went to see H. and M. and was just interrupted by a two-hour-long visit from the latter. I will continue the visits tomorrow and plan to stay here for a week before we visit Philadelphia, etc., according to plan.

For today adieu and a thousand greetings,

Yours, Ernst

As a postscript I need to report that my sense of republican virtue (if such existed in my head after I left Cato and school behind) suffered a hard jolt with our entry into the New World as detailed above. The customs officer who was inspecting my suitcase stood there comfortably, opening his hand behind his back saying: "You shan't have any trouble, Sir!"—which I answered silently but pleasantly with a few dollars. The noble republican immediately signed my luggage with chalk, meaning that the bags were properly "fixed." Our delay was due to Ernst, who had stored the presents in his suitcase and as a conscientious lawyer was not willing to seek refuge in such dreadfully corrupt practices.

5th Avenue Hotel
New York, June 11, 1869

I still feel strange when I write *New York* at the head of my letters and notice with every step on the street or even from my room into the corridor of the hotel that I am far, far away. New York is a brilliant place. Even though there is nothing to see here, it is hard to describe what all one *can* see. There are no galleries, no museums, no palaces. But the customs, the street life, the position and layout of the city would take more time to study properly and in detail than Dresden with its gallery, Venice with the Accademia, or other cities where works of art fascinate our interest in the same way that material products do here.

You've already known for ages that in New York, trade and financial gain, in short money, play the central role. First money, then money again, then, far behind, everything else. Any hint of poetry, if it ever existed here, is banned. The utilitarian principle reigns in its crassest form. Everything is measured by it; all things are classified by their material worth; even people are no exception. If we could talk in numbers and call our children according to their ages, 1, 2, and 3, instead of Karl or Eduard, the New Yorkers would surely start that custom. After all, they have started with the streets already; only the ones in the oldest part of the city have names. In most of the city, the streets are planned to run parallel and at right angles; the ones going west to east are called 1st, 2nd, and 3rd Street, the ones from south to north 1st, 2nd, and 3rd Avenue.

There are few exceptions to this uniform naming in the newer parts. One is the main street, Broadway, which cuts through the entire island lengthwise. I don't know how long this street is but would guess about a German mile [4.7 English miles]. It is the artery of New York, full of large hotels and huge stores of a kind we would not find in any European city, not even Paris or London. On Broadway, but especially on the streets around the harbor, the pulse of life is surprising and deafening even to someone like me, used to life in London City. You must have a good impression of this from my last letter. The busiest street in London compared to Broadway is like our Friedrichsstrasse compared to one of London's. People and conveyances are everywhere. Speaking of people, in London City we say that "business" is written on their faces. That is true here. There is nothing but business. On Broadway, Wall Street, Nassau Street, and others, no one looks around—they all push and shove through the crowd. Everyone acts according to the American principle of "get ahead" and the even more accepted principle that the shortest path between two points is a straight line, an eagerly practiced principle that leads to frequent collisions.

Ernst and I are having great trouble walking slowly so we can look at things comfortably. When we stop we get screamed at by three or four omnibus drivers urging us to ride along. These omnibuses drive along Broadway in immense numbers, almost one every half-minute, often several in a row. Horse trams are used in the other streets. Droshky carriages don't exist, and that's inconvenient for foreigners since we have to do a lot of walking and in this heat cannot manage much in a day. It is possible to hire a cab at the large plazas or at livery stables, but they are so expensive that one thinks three times before using them. Since personal freedom and any other kind are so pervasive, there are no tariffs posted, or at least no one checks them. If we don't agree on a price with the driver before starting, we are lost. And how much do such agreements help? On the memorable morning when we left the *Scotia*, after much bargaining and harassment we managed to find a cab to bring us to the hotel for $8.00 (I had managed to bring down the price by $2), hardly an hour's drive. These drivers, the roughest and most impudent riffraff, of course feel equal to any intellectual and gentleman and show it by their manners. I am convinced the fellow was thinking he was doing us a favor by taking us to the hotel for $8.00. The horse-drawn trams are much in use. Our city councilors could learn that they are useful even in busy streets like those here without hindering traffic, if the coach drivers knew what they were about. Almost every street has a tram. It is a fact that they don't cause more accidents than any other conveyance. For other vehicles, however, the tracks are not helpful: the carts jolt into the tracks and out of them; on the other hand the average street surface is so atrocious that one is shaken regardless, just as on the ocean.

The Broadway omnibuses are characteristic of American thrift. There are no conductors; they are too expensive. The only official is the driver. He usually sits outside, high on the coach box, and holds a line connected to the back door and threaded along the ceiling of the vehicle. This way he notices when someone gets on or off. You pay through a hole in the ceiling. If you want to get off you pull the line. If you don't pay right away he sounds a bell. Certainly practical!

The omnibuses and horse trams called streetcars are used by the most elegant ladies because they are the only form of conveyance available short of a horse-drawn carriage. Speaking of ladies, I must mention that they have a position in society which has little in common with our European concept. You might say that here a gentleman is chaperoned by a lady, not the other way around as is our custom. Here a lady may do anything, may go anywhere, may mix indiscriminately without running the danger of being insulted. Young girls walk around on Broadway or in the park by themselves or with young men of their acquaintance. They let themselves be picked up by said young men to take a drive in an open coach, or to go to the theater, or the favorite, to go to church. They breakfast alone in the dining rooms of the hotel and eat dinner there by themselves also. It happens for example that a lady will sit on the lap of a gentleman if the omnibus is full. In short the ladies act as if the gentlemen were lifeless pieces of wood or by nature "subordinate beings" who neither could nor would have the nerve to do something to them. What would be considered dangerous or at least reprehensible for our ladies is not thought to be so here. While we are speaking of women's emancipation, here one thinks occasionally of men's emancipation. An American lady in Europe may be even more puzzled by the behavior of us men than we are by their men here. A young girl may without embarrassment start a conversation with a young man. If one of them acts silly, with downcast eyes, it is decidedly not the girl.

As concerns the clothing of these ladies, it is beyond what I have ever seen. It is absolutely impossible to dress up more than American ladies do. There is no young girl, wealthy or poor, who does not follow the fashion. Right now broad sashes, conspicuously cut clothes, thick, high hairstyles, and magnificent shoes are the order of the day. Most of these girls are strikingly beautiful, delicate, and graceful and to me seem to combine the advantages of the English and French without any of their shortcomings. Their exaggerated elegance does not seem suited to New York.

As already mentioned, New York is no city of sky-high palaces, broad streets, beautiful promenades, etc. The houses are mostly built of red brick, have three or four front windows, and are on the low side. The English design, with an area in front, tends to predominate. Almost all streets are lined on both sides with trees that give shade but hide the character of a big city even more. Only on Broadway and 5th Avenue (from 14th Street up) are there exceptions to this. You see the huge hotels (ours, for instance, can house 800 people), then the colossal stores and a few big accounting houses. Most of the latter are on Wall Street at the southern end of the city, in the business district. Fifth Avenue has the magnificent houses of the elite who set the tone. Our hotel at the intersection of Broadway and 5th Avenue is, like many of the most elegant homes, built of white marble. This material is the only thing in proper relation to the dress code. The city is busy improving the layout with parks. The park called Central Park, which extends from 60th Street to the north, will eventually, when the newly planted trees have matured and are able to give shade, become a place of relaxation with no equal in the world.

Life in the best hotels is worthy of attention and possibly imitation by Europeans. We pay a certain sum for room and board per day, in the eastern part of the city, usually $5, regardless of whether we eat there or somewhere else. In this price range the rooms are not very cozy. They are on the 3rd or 4th floor and are furnished with hardly anything but bed and wash stand. If you choose to have more luxury, like comfortable chairs and sofas, and stay on the 1st or 2nd floor, you have to pay at least $6–7. Even then it might be hard to find a place on the lower floors because the first floor is taken up with drawing rooms, lavishly furnished halls for everyone's use. The second floor is usually reserved for large local families who, according to custom, often live in the hotels for years instead of renting apartments or owning their own houses. It is more convenient for the "housewives"!

Breakfast is usually served from 7:00–11:00, lunch from 1:00–2:00, dinner from 5:30–7:30, tea from 8:30–9:30, supper from 11:00–12:00. Within these hours you can order meals. You sit at small tables and choose as many courses from the menu as you like. These menus offer everything and more than everything—all the well-known foods I have ever heard of as well as many unknown national foods. For instance, today we had coconut pie for dessert. Wine has to be paid for but is hardly ever consumed at the table. In the enormous dining hall a waiter stands behind almost every chair, obeying the smallest sign. For me, such attention is almost too much; the fellows watch you put every bite into your month and that is uncomfortable. If, however, you need something at a different time or have an errand, it is hardly possible even with repeated requests and a little cry for "help." Boots are rarely found well cleaned in front of the door in the morning. With clothes it is "help yourself." The "gentlemen" waiters and houseboys are above such lowly tasks. Long live equality!

We see large numbers of black, brown, red-brown people, mulattos, and mestizos. Half the coachmen, especially the private vehicle drivers, are Colored, and many of the servants, maids, nurses, and workmen also. Ernst and I are planning to buy a little pickaninny and bring him to Europe as our servant. Don't be surprised if you see us appear in such company!

I am astounded at how well the New Yorkers manage to prepare their houses against great heat and cold alike. Right now you would think that New York is a city that would freeze to death if the thermometer dipped below 0 degrees Celsius. But friends tell me that they often have to endure truly Siberian temperatures.

Now everyone is dressed as lightly as possible. The employees in the accounting houses and in many stores wear shirt sleeves. In the houses, everything is open and it is impossible to find a spot without a draft. The windows of the omnibuses have no panes. In the hallways of the big hotels we enjoy the cool stone floors. Many houses have green blinds and enclosed balconies. Verandas decorated with greens and flowers lead down to the street. All this is just right for the warm temperature. Today was a hot day for June. Yesterday, in contrast, it was quite cool. On the day of our arrival the morning was rather pleasant. *Variatio delectat*, but I think the variation will soon cease and the heat will stay. The culinary delights are also adjusted to this heat: we can have ice water with everything and everywhere. Instead of tea one drinks milk with ice. And the Yankees are famous for mixing wine and stronger alcohol with ice not just for dinner, but at all times of the day, drinking these in large quantities while standing in bars. Sherry cobblers, mint juleps, cocktails, brandy smashes, and whatever else they may be called are all offered along with ice cream and iced lemonade in bars as well as at all street corners. That is also very foreign to us.

So much for today about "things." Now a few words about the people I have met so far. We have found Dr. A.,[5] whom you remember from the past and who is now the most famous of the local eye specialists. We found him to be a very gracious person. He and his brother received us warmly and both do what they can for us. They show us New York, explain everything, give us good advice for the rest of our trip by train to the interior of the country, provide us with introductions to friends in various places, introduce us to their German club. In short they are behaving in a most friendly and useful way. Last night they took us along to a party of German doctors where I felt quite at home. People sat together, drank wine, smoked, and chatted about politics just like us![6] *Berlin en Amerique!*

B. is an important acquaintance.[7] My letter of introduction to him was probably more useful than all the others. B. is the number one person in New York, so to speak. As leader of the Democratic Party, he enjoys a prestige that should in fact be incompatible with a republic. This does seem to have been going on for a very long time, though, and it is hard to say whether his party will win again in the coming elections. The Republican element seems to grow stronger roots in New York. When we went to visit him the day before yesterday, I left my card attached to the letter since he was not at home. On the next day there was a horse race near New York which seemed interesting to me and to which I drove even though I did not have high expectations, having just witnessed the Epsom Races.[8] B. is president of the Jockey Club, so I was hoping to run into him out there. He entered no less than 5 horses on that day, and he has 11 altogether, as he told me later. I found him, as expected, in the middle of the track, surrounded by a crowd which was congratulating him (he had just won the first race) and introduced myself. He took me along and showed me the entire race course, gave me a membership card in the Jockey Club for the next few days, and asked if he could be of use in any way, or whether I needed recommendations. Since I assented he sent me a packet of recommendations yesterday for St. Louis, Chicago, and all the big cities, even a special one for President Grant.

The latter is of course most interesting to me. My worry is whether I will have the opportunity to run into him. He is not in Washington now, but on a vacation trip on the Hudson. Next week the big Peace Festival[9] will be held in Boston, which you might have read about in the papers. Since he is planning to attend, it is doubtful that he will have returned to Washington by the time we are planning to be there. By the way, we might actually also be going to Boston since the dizzying spectacle to be enacted there supposedly will outdo anything ever done before. Among other things, there will be one (or several) musical performances. It is only unclear whether 20,000 or 30,000 people will participate. Sections of Uncle's[10] *Elijah* and *Paulus* [oratorios] are to be part of the repertoire so that it seems fitting to have a member of our family attend this extraordinary event. The only thing that might prevent our attendance is, as rumor would have it, that the hotels are all booked up. A.[11] has written to a friend about offering us lodging. We expect an answer tomorrow morning. Should it be positive, we will change our travel plans and visit Boston now rather than later. All our acquaintances advise it.

Adieu dear family. Ernst sends his greetings. He makes desperate attempts at writing, but can't quite get around to it. I assume you will share this and that from my letters with his family. I promised him I would report for both of us. We lead a merry life, eat with friends, drink with them, walk around with them, and have more than enough social obligations. We are never alone.

Parker House[12]
Boston, June 15, 1869

I am very pleased that we decided to come here! When A's friend Dr. Joy Jeffries, who lives in Boston, telegraphed us that he had reserved rooms in this hotel from which I am writing to you now, the question of our excursion was decided. To travel from New York to Boston we have a choice of two or three rail lines, some half train/half steamship. The latter are supposed to be more pleasant because of the variety, but it turned out that the cabins on the boats had all been spoken for since Friday so that we had to settle for the nine-hour-long train journey. The travel to Boston being so booked already may give you a sense of the crowds expected here.

This was my first trip by American train, a curious enough experience to deserve a few words of description. In New York, we drove to the station on 24th Street and sat down in the train that was waiting without a locomotive. On a signal each car is pulled by four horses to the more distant train station on 42nd Street. Once there, a locomotive of strange-looking construction is added to the reconstituted train. Especially noticeable is an iron frame across the front of the engine which almost reaches down to the tracks and is called a cowcatcher. As the name implies, this thing is specially designed to push cows that run around in great numbers, close to and on the tracks, out of the way. During the trip we often saw animals, hurled away thus, dying next to the tracks; when one inspects the cowcatcher at the next stop it is spattered with blood.

Only a few days ago such a necessary slaughter of an innocent creature almost cost President Grant his life: The train he took had just hurled away a cow that rolled back down an incline onto the tracks and separated the last two cars from the rest. The last two, in which the presidential party was traveling, escaped with no more than a fright and a monumental jolt while the other cars derailed, resulting in many deaths and injuries. Despite all this the cowcatcher is useful and indispensable for the security of the passengers. The train tracks are not closed off: they run through cities, gardens, and promenades without ceremony, hardly ever on a causeway, but usually on a level with the streets.

The tracks are often used as a comfortable place to take a walk, so that not only cows, horses, and other animals but also people occasionally give the cowcatcher work. There are no barriers where the tracks cut through streets, only a simple sign saying: "Crossing the line, please look out for the engine." Everyone has to watch out for himself. To my consternation I would often witness small children calmly playing close to the tracks. Except for the cowcatcher, no other security measures exist for the traveler. Track men are not even known by name. It is well known that the newspapers report many accidents daily. Thus the insurance business on trains flourishes. Agents of the various insurance companies often follow you almost all the way into the train, listing all the accidents of the last week and cold-bloodedly telling you that your chances of breaking your neck are one in a hundred, thus urging you to be mindful of your family.

The cars are built differently from ours, more like in the Swiss system. Since there is only one class there are no compartments. Each car has a big open space with many rows of benches divided in the middle, leaving room to pass. We sit two to a bench, none too comfortably. There are two large stoves in each car for the winter. Passenger movement from one car to the next is continual, even while the train is moving. A boy passes every few minutes, bringing complimentary ice water. People selling newspapers, books, candy, and fruit, as well as distributing advertisements, move back and forth. Before getting off at the stops, one has to be careful to find out how long the train is scheduled to stay in the station. This is not easy, however, because the train officials don't wear uniforms and it is hard to find someone to ask.

Americans detest anything to do with uniforms. They suspect their freedom is limited by officials. On the Erie train (the only company requiring its employees to wear little insignia) it supposedly was difficult to get such signs accepted. For the same reason, even mailmen and policemen have only had a recognizable uniform for a short while. It is certainly a nuisance for the public that the executive officials can't be recognized as such.

Parts of the trip to Boston are marvelously beautiful: the train crosses numerous rivers, on wooden bridges, be it added; what a relief to get over them without incident! Especially the Connecticut River offers beautiful views. The vegetation is rather lush, moderately high mountains covered by thick woods. The countryside is quite populated and built up. What caught my attention is that everything seems finished only far enough to hold together or be serviceable. Streets are only partly or incompetently paved, some are still dirty and swampy, others partly sandy; houses of all kinds and constructions stand next to each other, many made of wood or half-timbered, hardly any built of brick. In the cities these houses are often moved from one place to the next at the whim of the owner who wants a different neighborhood or surroundings, while the inhabitants calmly remain inside. On Staten Island, the other day, I saw a house of dimensions close to ours in Charlottenburg on such a trip; supposedly in Chicago this wandering habit is most common and changes the look of entire neighborhoods.

We stopped for half an hour toward evening (our train was an express train and moved at great speed) in order to let the travelers have dinner. There was no restaurant at the station, so that we had to find a nearby hotel. We spent half the time running around trying to find one so we did not have much time to eat. We arrived here rather starved.

Our hotel is just as busy as the one in New York. There is a sign announcing operation "on the European plan" [in English in the original], but all that means is that we pay separately for the meals while the "American style," as you know, is to pay for lodging and meals together. Indeed, everything in this hotel is typically American: the lordliness of the servants, the public reading room that anyone from the street can enter, a salon on the ground floor where dandified gentlemen sit at large windows and inspect the passing ladies, etc.

The city is very handsome. They say here that money reigns in New York, blood in Boston. That means that name and descent are important here, while in New York one is "worth" so and so many thousand dollars. Here, if someone is related to an old English family, they are proud of it and will on all occasions draw attention to it. Boston is the oldest city in the US. Its society is famous for appreciating knowledge, erudition, and the arts. Americans in general look upon Massachusetts with a kind of pride. The city is less spread out than New York, not accounting for the considerable difference in population (300,000 compared to one million). The reason may be that almost all the houses are built into the bay on stilts and the construction therefore had to be less wasteful of space and closer together. Now that the city is growing more on the mainland also, more suburbs are being built toward the west. Among the several buildings we saw today I must mention the public library, possessing about half a million books and owing its founding capital to a Mr. Bates who used to be an associate of the London Barings.[13] Anyone in good civil standing may pick up books there, certainly a beneficial liberality. Here as in many public buildings and institutes, the officials are of the female gender. To my enjoyment, they wear quite elegant clothes, rather out of place at their job!

Another wonder is a "baby show," which we went to see this evening. At this point there were only 25 to 30 babies; often there are 300–400 children aged 1–5 on display. The whole affair is the enterprise of one man; he pays the parents of each child a certain sum and gives a prize to the best dressed and healthiest child. The entrepreneur receives enough from the entrance fees of visitors that he usually comes out with a distinct profit. The well-dressed children play in a big hall, looking lively and sweet. Remarkably, the visitors were almost exclusively young men!

At 3:00 we attended the festive opening of the "National Peace Jubilee."[14] The festival is supposed to last for five days, with a big concert each day, and a ball on Thursday. I now have the musical program in front of me and realize that in addition to excerpts from *Paulus* and *Elijah*, two of Uncle's psalms are also to be sung. Only shorter pieces of music, overtures, arias, etc. are performed, no larger works. Among many others the overture to *Freischütz* is ascribed to Mozart![15] For this festival, the city had a building erected which can accommodate 60,000 people, not counting the musicians. These musicians consist of a chorus of more than 20,000 singers, an orchestra of 1,094 instruments, and three music directors. An imposing organ was built especially for this hall. In addition, 300 firemen hammer on their anvils at a certain place in Verdi's *Trovatore*, an effect that fits Verdi's music rather well. Finally 12 cannons were stationed outside with their pilot lights connected to an electric battery near the main conductor. Someone would press a button on this battery at the right moment, to set off a cannon and make the entire building shake. What do you think of a concert like that?

To the disappointment of the entire audience, President Grant, despite the original promise, is not expected here until tomorrow, so that someone else had to open the ceremony. First there was a prayer, then two speeches, according to the program: one to welcome the guests, the other to glorify peace (I did not understand one word of either). Then the music started with Luther's "God is a castle and defense" [sic in source], *Ein' feste Burg ist unser Gott*. Then came the overture to *Tannhäuser*, the Gloria of Mozart's twelfth Mass, several national anthems, Rossini's overture to *Tell*, etc. The solo, Ave Maria by Gounod, sung by Madame Parepa-Rosa, was accompanied by 200 violins. The performance was exemplary and could not have been better. Not the smallest inadequacy in orchestra or chorus could be noticed; strangely the soft parts were especially remarkable. The solo by Madame Parepa, who had already pleased me with her beautiful voice in a concert in New York, was the achievement of an artist of the first rank. Altogether this side of the ocean does not seem to lack in good music and excellent performers to present it. Beside the concert I just mentioned, which was held in Steinway Hall (home of the local choral society), and which was attended by the more sophisticated public, I attended a concert in Central Park, conducted by a certain Thomas (a German like most of the musicians), comparable to our "Liebig'sche Concerte."[16] The playing there was also excellent. A cornet soloist by the name of Levy deserves special mention; the artistic execution was of the first rank. I can't say the same about the taste of the audience, which the artists unfortunately gratify. The eagerness with which this music festival is being supported can be seen by the fact that each state sends a contingent of singers for the chorus; New York alone sent 500 ladies and gentlemen.

The crush of the crowd was enormous. Today's price for tickets to Thursday's ball is already $8; the original price was $2. Elegant clothes everywhere, mostly worn by people from out of town; the calm, aristocratic locals do not like the hurly-burly and many have left the city earlier than usual for the summer vacation. The temperature in the hall was downright tropical, but it is not much different on the streets. The combination of the rather strong rainfall of the last few days and the heat make it undesirable to be outside. Of course the cloudy sky and the rain do help with the heat, and so far the evenings are cool and the nights refreshing.

We went to visit Dr. Joy Jeffries, who had arranged our lodging. He prepared a complete plan of what we need to see while here and will accompany us to a few places himself. A Mr. Lincoln, also recommended to us, offered his friendly services in addition. In short we are so well taken care of again that I have no opportunity to use my official letters of introduction. I would rather save the time. It is very pleasant how obliging people are. And doubtless I will have the pleasure of more than one opportunity to make a similar report.

Exchange Hotel[17]
Richmond (Va.), June 19, 1869

As on my travels last summer,[18] I have come to the point at which I am in despair about all that I would like to tell you. You know that I can't rest till I have made you participate in my joys. The only saving grace is journal style, which serves as short reminders for future oral reports.

My previous letter contained fleeting descriptions of events through Tuesday June 15. On Wednesday morning we had the pleasure of seeing the President join the Boston Peace festivities. How different are the European customs for receiving a head of state! Instead of the military there was a civilian militia preceding Grant, but no other sign of anything extraordinary. He sat in street clothing with a cigar in his mouth—I understand he is never seen without one—with three other gentlemen in an open carriage, the private vehicle of a rich rental agent, and was chauffeured by the proprietor himself. The latter was also casually dressed. Behind this official "state carriage" some rented vehicles followed with many men accompanying the President, interspersed with the usual horse trams and other vehicles. The houses had already hung flags for the festivities the day before and large crowds (strangers and locals in equal numbers) had already observed the proceedings yesterday. So nothing was especially meant for the person of the President. Stores and businesses were closed for the entire week, with everyone milling around.

Another example of how crowded things are may be of interest to you: On Wednesday Ernst and I had to wait for half an hour at the door of the dining room of our own hotel before we could enter—it was that busy. Someone kept the door cordoned off with a chain and only admitted as many people as left, even though this hall is about twice as big as Uncle A's in Jägerstraße.[19]

On the same afternoon the President held a parade of 6,000 militia. We watched them march past. Everything was about as unmilitary as possible. One soldier wore a dark red uniform, the next a light red one with many shades in between. A drummer unapologetically wore a straw hat. The kettle drummer had a street urchin help him carry the instrument, which no doubt had become too heavy for him. The republican officers made a conservative impression with their broad-brimmed, droopy felt hats and colorful drooping feathers, and the heavy harness of their horses was like what used to be hung on battle chargers in the old days. They might well have found all this in a used goods store at a reduced price.

We were especially interested in a Negro battalion with Negro officers, sutlers, etc. The fellows looked rather grotesque, and I will always remember the image of their major with his big tummy dancing along on his thin short horse. In the evening we enjoyed the spectacle of the fire brigade with their machines lit up by stick lanterns. The American fire brigade is known to be the model for ours. Their look is beyond reproach and their handling of the recently invented steam jet (also used in England) is said to deserve the same compliment.

After this spectacle we attended the theater, where we saw the popular comedian Lingard, who performed for us striking impressions of famous people. He mentioned a few characteristic words with each person he presented. When it came to President Grant, he brought out a burning cigar, kept it in his mouth, and stayed silent. Both these references to the president's habits, always smoking, never speaking, earned strong applause. The police not only tolerate this but President Grant was invited to the performance. It seems that Grant is not beloved by either party. He is not Republican enough for the ones who helped elect him and they all say that he is insignificant and even lazy. The newspapers express skepticism and impudence regarding him. I saw one yesterday which said: "It seems wonderful that a person like the President, who looks like nothing special, has attracted so large a crowd," and more of this kind. Another paper said: "Yesterday Grant came through such and such place. The municipal officials greeted him at the station. The president did not answer and smoked two cigars." [the last sentence is in English] A personal description of the President will follow after I have been introduced to him in Washington. Chances are good that I will meet him when I get there.

Thursday morning we took a long ride through the area and the suburbs of Boston despite the heat. We went through Charleston, past Bunker Hill, where they erected a monument to the bygone battle;[20] through Cambridge, where there is a university for the education of American youth and where we saw Longfellow's[21] house; through Mount Auburn, which is a beautifully arranged cemetery used by the Bostonians as a promenade. We only returned to the city at 3:00 in the afternoon. We passed many pretty country mansions, almost all built of wood. We saw similar ones on the island of Nahant, which, as I forgot to mention, we visited on Wednesday afternoon, traveling for one very worthwhile hour by steamship from Boston harbor.

In great spirits, due to the success of our excursion, we returned to New York on Thursday afternoon, traveling the other route: First we rode the train for two hours to Newport, a favorite watering place for New Yorkers. We traveled very pleasantly in a so-called state saloon, a luxuriously appointed car for six people which costs a bit more than the usual ticket price. This attempt to separate the better and richer population from the others only exists on certain lines so far and is lucrative for the coffers of the company so that no doubt it will be imitated on other lines also. To avoid bad blood they don't call it first and second class. Given the heat this offering is splendid and we will use it wherever it is available. The infamous American habit of constantly spitting (which I will eventually describe in a separate chapter) is as disgusting on trains as everywhere else. At least in the state saloons, there are spittoons that keep the mess from the carpet or wooden floor.

Arriving in Newport at 7:00 we immediately boarded the steamship that was to take us to New York by the next morning. I must tell you about this steamship. It does not correspond in anything to the concept a European would have of a trip made on something called a ship. Imagine a four-story building that floats, each floor having a gallery around it on which one can sit; no mast, no rigging of any kind; above the roof which covers the top floor protrude a couple of narrow chimneys, and two enormous paddle boxes are working on the sides. That's what the thing looks like from the outside. The inside is not as easy to describe.

As we entered, a number of Negroes came running in to take our things and show us the bedroom which we had reserved in Boston and to which the conductor had handed us the key on the train. First we had to work our way through a chaos of boxes, chests, bales of stuff, skins, cattle, and travelers' suitcases. Then we climbed two floors on a staircase as broad as the one leading to our entryway in Charlottenburg[22] and two salons of a size and height which I don't think any of our acquaintances command. The stairs are lit with bronze candelabra, the halls with golden gas chandeliers. Comfortable chairs and sofas, divans, game tables, and marble tables are everywhere, all on thick carpets. These two halls, which are on the top two floors only and function as music halls, have galleries around them holding stands for the orchestra, and are lined by the doors to the bedrooms. The evening concert accompanying each trip lasts only from 8–10 so that people are not disturbed later on in their sleep. The bedrooms, "staterooms," are very elegant; the beds, two in each stateroom, are of the same size as ours in Germany, with the most beautiful lace curtains. The windows have curtains and Venetian blinds. Carpets like in England are a matter of course. The first glimpse of all this shocked Ernst and me more than anything else on this trip, and we were "speechless for five minutes" like Carl M. in Venice. Having recovered from our amazement we completed our inspection. People had already gathered in the music halls. We received printed programs and took a seat on the abovementioned plush furniture that made the auditorium look more like a social gathering. The performance was excellent, but the program was awful. We listened for a while, then went downstairs. There were two more salons furnished as drawing rooms. As in the music rooms, many doors led to the outside and were kept open so that the refreshing coolness from the water could stream in. We went down another floor to find a dining hall the size of two normal ones, but the ceiling was not as high. Before entering, we passed a coatroom where we left hat and coat with a Negro; to the left were a toilet and washroom for men, together with barber and shaving facilities, also run by blacks. The dining room was organized like a buffet in the finest hotels; the menu showed all manner of meals, and about twenty Negroes in white were busy as waiters. I felt like Papageno among the masses.

You would have to see such a ship to believe it. We stayed up till 11, partly in the halls, partly on the galleries, and then went to bed. I awoke at 5 just as we passed between the islands of Manhattan and Long Island, looking at the houses farthest north of New York on the one side and a row of beautiful villas on the other. The East River, the arm of the Hudson encircling Manhattan on the east, was quite busy already. We saw mostly steamships whose fast pace gave the impression of busyness, like most activities in and around New York. The innumerable steam ferries which New York maintains regularly with its suburbs Hoboken, Jersey, and Brooklyn, each of which has room for 1,500 people and the corresponding number of carriages and horses, were already running.

We landed at 6 o'clock. Since we were planning to continue our trip here in the evening we did not book a hotel but instead spent the day in the city. Among other activities we attended a juried court (juries are used for civil cases here also) where a lady was accused of not paying a dental bill. By the way, for the uninitiated, it is impossible to tell the difference between judge, jury, witnesses, accused, and public. They sit right on top of each other. Then we went to the biggest of the clothing stores I already mentioned in my first letter, which is one of the many Gersons[23] in New York, belonging to a Mr. Stuart who recently refused a nomination as a Cabinet secretary and is rumored to be one of the richest men in America. The building is possibly three times as large as our Gerson.[24] Standing on the ground floor one can look up six stories. The building takes up most of an entire street block and is made of white marble.

At 8 in the evening, we took a ferry across the Hudson to get to the express train in Jersey which took us to Washington. On this trip, sleeping cars were a novelty to us; they have recently become the norm on overnight trips. The tickets for these sleeping cars can be bought like regular tickets, ahead of time (even several days ahead), at special offices all over town or from a specific official at the station. These sleeping cars have broad, comfortable seats during the day that get converted into clean and well-upholstered beds in the evening, always two, one above the other, like on ships. Gentlemen and ladies are not separated, and each set of two is only divided by a full-length curtain. The middle of the carriage has a corridor which at both ends turns into a small room with washing utensils, towels and a mirror, even comb and brush for the enthusiast. One of these is usually used by the gentlemen, the other by the ladies. But they frequently get mixed up also. The half-dressed figures gathering there would seem not so much "American" as "Spanish" to a young lady of our country.

A room for undressing does not exist. One takes off one's outer clothes in the hallway and finishes by putting on sleepwear in bed. A Negro servant detailed to the car helps, brushing out clothes, cleaning boots, and altogether trying to create the illusion that we are staying in a hotel. We spent the night in such a carriage and, considering the unusual bedroom (we had procured a stateroom) and the constant movement, slept quite well. Of course it was hot. When we arrived in Washington at 6:00 in the morning we felt very little of the usual bleary-eyed state normal after a night on a train.

In Washington, we left the train and spent three hours on the Potomac River, which below Washington becomes as broad as a lake. At Acquia Creek, a small stop at the border of Virginia, we took the train again. It is possible to stay on the train from Washington to Richmond, but that is a considerable detour so everyone prefers the cooler, more interesting steamship on the Potomac. Among other places, we passed Washington's famous burial place at Mount Vernon. While passing, the ship's bell is rung as a sign of deference.

I saw practically nothing during the trip from New York to Washington because I was asleep. The little I saw seemed to confirm Karl's[25] judgment that it is an "unimportant area." Virginia, through which we traveled, starting from Acquia Creek, is sparsely farmed and has suffered terribly from the war. For both of us, this state is of great interest because it is one of the most important southern ones we will see. At first glance it is not attractive. The train stations are like stables, with no food to be had until Richmond except for some eggs and fruit here and there. The only thing in great abundance is Negroes. At 2:30 in the afternoon we arrived in great heat. The thermometer showed 27.5°R[26] in the shade at 6:00 p.m.

The impression Richmond makes is so strange and characteristic that I would not have wanted to miss it for anything in the world and am glad that at the last moment we added it to our travel plans. As the capital of the Confederacy, which was terminated by the horrible war four years ago, as the capital of a slave state, and as the territory of the most violent and bloody battles of this century, it differs considerably from the two big northern cities which we have seen so far. Richmond with its 40,000 inhabitants is a spread-out place, half city, half village. We were struck by the enormous number of Negroes, which almost seems to match the number of whites in this place. On our way to the hotel we drove through parts of the city where we did not see a single white face.

Sunday 20th, continuation

Only Negro children were playing in the street and in an open market and a market hall; the busy life we saw unfolding involved exclusively black buyers and black sellers. The apartments in this part of Richmond are poor and dirty while there are many pretty, large, and even elegant houses in the main quarters of the whites. The war has left terrible traces, more even than in the flat country. Everywhere there are burned-out places and destroyed gardens. Trade is interrupted, the well-being of a large number of families undermined; many of the richest people are now practically beggars. One of the latter is a certain Mr. Valentine,[27] whom we visited at the recommendation of Professor von H. This man, a gentleman such as one finds frequently in the South, and rarely in the North, received us warmly, and is leading us around to see the sights. Most importantly he explains the social and political controversies in an intelligent way. Father will be interested in some of what he told us, so I will put some things down even if in a hurry and superficially.

Southerners and Northerners are still very bitter toward each other. The former consider the Northerners conquerors who ruined their interests, and despise the federation they were forced to join, while having lost all hope of ever being able to leave it again. The governor of Virginia,[28] a Northerner or "Yankee" as these are called in mockery, is the object of both political and personal hatred; nobody invites him or goes to see him; any Virginian family who interacted with him would be shunned by society. Our friend, who is a sculptor,[29] said he would not ask a Northerner to his house even on business; at the most he would deal with him in his studio. All "old Virginians," as he called them, would think the same.

The position of the two races with regard to each other is most interesting, and, in this context, so is the strange behavior of the Northerners, the flag-bearers of Negro emancipation. They show a rather greater contempt for their former protégés than the inhabitants of the former slave states. In the north as here, the Negroes travel in special train compartments, they drink the ice water offered at hotels, public places, and train stations available to everyone, but out of special cups; they sit in specified places in church; when they are witnesses at court proceedings and kiss the Bible as part of their oath they are presented with a different Bible from that of the white witnesses; they are not allowed on the omnibus or to sit in the good seats in the theater; they do not follow a trade of their own, but at best, one or the other of them has a little shop; the only profession for them is serving others. I notice that they have many habits still reminiscent of slavery, such as bowing to the ground when they thank you. Their women often dress like Europeans but as a result look awful in their green, red, or pink dresses; the little Amazon hats look repulsively ugly on their woolly heads. Wearing the uniform of a servant makes them look much better; then they add white turbans or big hats that project past the face for three to four inches and protect the neck with an extension in the back. Negro women often seem to be nannies; I have yet to see a white woman in that capacity on our travels.

The Negroes seem quite useful as servants; they are friendly and fast, do what you ask but without thinking, which may be best for a servant anyway. Waiters, cooks, maids are all Negroes in our hotel; I must add that I use this name for all nuances of dark skin from pitch black to the Indian copper red, excluding the last. I still find those fellows ridiculous. When such a black face with woolly hair, glaring white/yellow eyes, and thick lips asks me obsequiously what I would like for breakfast, I think I am on stage in a comedy. When they have brought the desired meal they stand behind my seat, using a big whisk fan to cool me off and to chase off insects. That is very pleasant. But I do feel like a plantation owner or slave breeder. You must admit it is a funny thought to see a city councilor[30] from Berlin being fanned by a black man.

The heat yesterday and today is extraordinary for a European. This morning at 6:30 my thermometer showed 35 degrees in the sun. In the afternoon at 3:30 in the shade it was 30 degrees.[31] As soon as I reach the hotel I sit completely unclothed and still sweating. Pity me and excuse this bad letter.

Like all houses here the hotel is prepared for great heat and the rooms are relatively cool. The courtyard, planted with greenery, is surrounded by a gallery of lovely shady plazas where crowds of idle strangers and locals present the observing eye with a varied selection of eccentric postures. In the middle is a pretty fountain, just as one imagines in the Orient. Men and women walk around with fans. In the evening they sit on the stone steps of their houses, the ladies in light summer dresses, very pretty to watch. Before sundown we don't walk, but are transported by a Negro driver. Today we took a long ride from 8:00 in the morning to 3:30 in the afternoon, to and across the battlefield, saw the churchyards where the soldiers are buried, and brought bullets back with us; they are still lying around everywhere. It was a worthwhile and entertaining trip; our driver, who had been in the fire himself, was a splendid guide. He explained the positions of the army and the progress of the battle "almost like a human" as one is supposedly allowed to say in a slave state. Attractions in the city include the house of the former President of the Confederacy, Jefferson Davis, also the present government building which is called the Capitol as in all the other states and in which the legislature convenes every year.* (It also contains a complete and usefully arranged library.) There is a very handsome statue of Washington and finally the Holywood cemetery that delighted me even more than Mount Auburn in Boston. We drove there yesterday in brilliant moonlight and the sparkle of great swarms of fireflies. We had a good view of Richmond and the James River from the cemetery yesterday as well as from Gambles Hill today. This hill is a favorite evening walk of the Richmond ladies, beauties promenading in the moonlight without hats,

---

* The next summer, just as the legislators were assembled in the Great Hall on the second floor, the floor collapsed and half of the persons gathered there fell to the floor below. About 50 were killed and more were wounded. That shows how solidly the thing was built!

armed just with fans. It is rural and "southern." Later we took a look at the church where a service was going on after 9:00 p.m. because of the heat. The Americans keep their Sundays holy almost as strictly as the English, so the building was completely full. To keep the heat to a minimum the gas was turned down during the sermon—very practical. The sexton did not wear official attire but made himself comfortable in an ordinary linen jacket without a vest. I was sitting on the balcony near an open window, looking out at the stars and the dark trees of St. Paul's Church square during the singing. It was an unforgettable hour.

Tomorrow Valentine[32] will show us a tobacco factory. Tobacco is of first importance for trade here; we have seen large fields cultivated with this noble plant. This trade seems to be the only one that is still extant since the war. We will pay a last visit to the club we were introduced to the day before yesterday. We made several pleasant acquaintances there (all Americans. The approximately 1,000 Germans here are all of a lower class). Later we will eat at Valentine's mother's[33] before returning to Washington at night, which in this heat is more tolerable than during the day. We have been very well the whole time and are acclimating well. We rival the Americans in drinking ice water. If that would only stop the endless thirst which plagues us despite all the streams we pump into ourselves!

Continental Hotel[34]
Philadelphia, June 24, 1869

The much-anticipated event happened as planned, and we had an audience with the President of the United States! I find it almost funny, but you can imagine how much joy it gave me. Before I engage the historical, however, I will produce a proof and ask you to look at the enclosed newspaper article that corroborates the great fact. It is rather interesting how quickly the journals obtain such reports. Our audience was at 11:00 and at 3:00, I bought this paper in our hotel.

Last Monday I sent you my previous letter from Richmond. That day was also extremely hot; at 5:30 in the morning, the thermometer showed 35°R in the sun. Nonetheless Mr. Valentine, whose extraordinary friendliness I can't stress enough, accompanied us on a quest for notable sights. We visited the abovementioned tobacco factory in which the entire workforce consisted of Negroes of both genders; the tobacco exchange; a flour mill (which is said to be the biggest in the world; what all don't the inhabitants of the American cities think of as the "biggest in the world"?); a brewery where we as strangers were offered free lager beer. Finally, we listened to a court proceeding in which four blacks sat in the dock. In addition to what I wrote earlier about blacks I will mention the following: When I entered the courtroom I saw that all the seats were occupied by blacks. I did not pay attention and was about to sit down among them when Valentine pulled me up almost in a panic as if the wooden bench was on fire and said: "Don't you see, there are only Negroes." We ended up sitting somewhere else among the attorneys and Valentine could hardly calm down about the "mistake" I almost committed. I did not care myself, of course. On the contrary, I find it amusing to interact with blacks. If they just did not look so much the same! I have a hard time remembering a specific physiognomy, but only recognize the general type in each. If, for instance 20 such fellows are serving in the dining room of a hotel, I can never remember which one belongs to me. I have confused things more than once by asking one for something I had not ordered from him.

Monday afternoon at 5:00, we attended the previously announced dinner party in our honor at Mrs. Valentine's.[35] Beside some friends of their son, both his sisters were present (one married, the other not), Mr. Valentine's brother[36]—who together with him spent four years in Berlin and has, like him, since been enamored of our city—and his brother-in-law. Before dinner, the men gathered in a separate room to partake of a punch made of pineapple and wine from Virginia. After half an hour, the ladies joined us and we took them to dinner, which was quite good and was served by blacks. Of the drinks, I must mention the champagne of California, more for its rarity than its quality. Had the temperature been a little more moderate, I would have amused myself excellently because the guests were most friendly and attentive to us. If I may judge by this sample, the better circles in Richmond consist of refined and educated people.

At 8:00, accompanied by the brothers Valentine, we proceeded directly from the party to the train station. We took the same route back to Washington, left the train at 1:00 at night, slept on board the Potomac steamer, and landed in Washington at 6:00 a.m. Soon after our arrival, we tried to visit Mr. von Krause,[37] our chargé d'affaires (Baron von Gerolt is in Europe at the moment). Since he was not at home, we hired a carriage from the hotel—walking is out of the question here too, because of the heat, even though it is not quite as intense as in Richmond—and had the black driver take us to "the most interesting places."

Seen from the outside, this city would certainly not live up to the expectations of any but a few people—and would disappoint them, as it did me. Only six buildings are imposing in style; they are surrounded by a few pretty houses, mostly inhabited by foreign ambassadors, and a cluster of big, ugly hotels. The rest looks like a farming village of huge dimensions.

We visited the six imposing buildings in the following order: 1) The White House (today only from the outside), which is the home of the President. Like all the other official buildings, it is made of white marble and is of simple construction, almost middle class. It is situated on a pretty little hill in the middle of a park, making a very noble impression despite its simplicity. 2) The War Department. 3) The Treasury Office. In neither of these is there a soldier on guard duty, nor is there any other security against intrusion by the general public. The rooms are open and one can look into almost all the offices. Mainly female office personnel seem to be working there. 4) The Patent Office, where models of inventions that are patented in the United States are on exhibit. Almost everything gets patented here. No wonder the huge building is almost completely filled with models. Since visitors would find it impossible to orient themselves among the numerous exhibits, they are asked upon entering whether they have a special request and are then taken to that area by a guide. 5) The General Post Office, generously constructed and designed for its purpose. 6) The Capitol, the government and legislative building of the United States— the most important and surely the most impressive building in America. It is very imposing even though some of the ornamentation on the outside is not quite finished yet. Maybe it's a little overdone, with its masses of marble. I would not know which architectural style to call it, but its size, which I believe tops that of the Vatican, lets you forget any deficiencies. Beside all kinds of courts, libraries, and administrative offices, it contains the chambers of the Senate and of the House of Representatives that we were especially curious about. Even though they are not as magnificently appointed as the English chambers, they are much more imposing than ours. They differ from the chambers of other nations in that the Senate and House of Representatives are adorned in the same way, while for instance the English Upper House is more imposing than the Lower House. Each member of Congress sits at a very comfortable desk; the public and journalists are also well provided for; in each chamber there is room for 1,500 people in the galleries. The President's two private rooms, one for work and the other for receptions, are appointed in a luxurious style with many pictures and much gold ornamentation. From the cupola of the building one can see the city, the suburb of Georgetown, and the surrounding areas, even though the view does not offer anything attractive.

Our final visit on Tuesday was to a government dock yard (called navy yard here) where war ships are built and equipped. We were especially fascinated with this establishment because it contained three of the "monitors," the American armored ships we had heard so much about during the Civil War. Through the personal intercession of the Admiral, who readily gave us permission without much ado, we were allowed to inspect them. However, after seeing one we did not care to tour the others. Like the English turret ships, this monitor is made entirely of iron; its surface only penetrates the water's surface by 1½ feet; the tower is a little higher, with enough room on it for the captain and two cannons. On the ship we inspected, those cannons were 600-pounders. The tower is the only protruding object on the surface of the 200-foot-long ship with a surface slanting from the middle to the sides, making it slippery to walk on. The monitor is a ship without sides. It has no deck to stand on. As soon as it moves, the entire crew of 100 men descends into the Underworld. There it is completely dark, with only one narrow port through which to crawl down. Daylight is so scarce that we had to be shown around with a light. It seems to me that a stay down there while on the high seas must be three times more horrible than the worst underground prison. It would feel like being caught in an iron pipeline.

Tuesday (*horribile dictu*) we went to bed at 9:00 because we were tired out. A carriage outing in an American city is not like in Berlin. The road surfaces there may be terrible, but nothing compared to the ones here. In Washington it may be even worse than in other cities. Sometimes the streets are all sand, sometimes clay where vehicles sink and pigs frolic; sometimes an unsuccessful attempt has been made to lay down pavement, but this makes things even worse because rattling over the deep holes and the terrible shaking make you feel seasick. No other vehicle gets preference except the horse-drawn trams that drive in the middle of the causeway and are used by everyone. As a rich man living in Washington, I would not think of keeping an equipage—it would be torture to drive around in it. In fact, I don't think anyone keeps a carriage; only tourists hire them, when they want to see as much as possible in a short time.

Since the city is extraordinarily spread out, the large distances require one to drive, despite the inconvenience, and they increase the cost of paving, which proceeds at a slow rate, if at all. As in other important cities, both sides of the streets are lined with shade trees. The population is similar to that of Richmond, the number of blacks being equally large.

While Congress is in session, many strangers attend in addition to the delegates, which explains why such an enormous number of hotels can exist right next to each other.

Wednesday morning we again visited Mr. v. K.,[38] whose return visit we had missed. He gave us useful information of all kinds and told us that at the suggestion of the Secretary of State he would give us whatever letters of introduction to consuls we might need in other states. We requested one each for St. Louis and San Francisco; these he will send after us. Then we checked on the formalities used in visiting the President and he gave us a card to Adjutant General Dent,[39] who might possibly help us should we not be granted an audience. This turned out to be unnecessary. The audiences being from 10:00–12:00 daily, we dressed in white trousers with black jacket and vest and were taken to the White House by our Negro at 11:00. There we were admitted to an anteroom on the first floor that was filled with people awaiting their turn. In the middle of the room, an administrative employee was sitting at a table writing down the names of the arrivals. It seems to me he also had the task of furnishing the press with the appropriate news items. I told this official that I had a personal introduction to the President and gave him our cards. He immediately gave those and B.'s letter to a black servant to take in to the President. We had not waited three minutes before the same servant came back and led us into the *sanctum sanctissimum*. What do you think about this preferential treatment? This distinction caused the others to eye us with irritable curiosity.

As we entered, two other gentlemen came in to deliver some papers before retreating again immediately. The President, dressed in black, was standing at his desk with the well-known never-missing cigar in his mouth.

The big room was furnished very sparsely. After we had bowed deeply he shook our hands, sat down, and invited us to have a seat. As we sat down he looked at us so pointedly that I was a little uneasy despite my usual cheeky self. Ernst, as he told me afterward, had the same reaction. Starting the conversation I gave a little speech in my best English about how happy we were to get to see him, etc. This he took with a gracious thank you and asked after our plans, how we were enjoying the States, relayed to us this and that about the country and its people, and finally talked a little about relations with Europe. As befitted well-bred Prussians, we responded in a brief and concise way and retired after about ten minutes, having thanked him for the extraordinary honor and shaken his hand once more. As we were leaving the room through one door five more people, two ladies included, entered through another. The poor man!

We then asked a servant to show us the staterooms, which are large and dignified, without pomp, but elegantly decorated. Then we took a little drive in our carriage ("after that scare" as Berliners would say), being well pleased with our visit to the White House. To have been admitted to the President was more than we could have hoped for, since Krause had told us that it was especially difficult to see him right now when he had just come back from a trip. On top of that, it is highly exceptional (Krause informed us) to get to see him alone.

Grant is a short man, hardly taller than I, squarely built with a blond full beard and blond hair, close to 50 years old. He speaks very softly. I was glad each time he asked a question and I could understand it. He is relatively monosyllabic in conversation and as with many people who speak little, it is hard to tell whether he does not know how to talk or simply does not care to. He is certainly not, by the way, an insignificant man, as his opponents claim. It can have been no small matter to play such a role in the war. In an ironic turn of events we were next driven to the former residence of General Lee, Grant's most important opponent. The house has been confiscated, and Lee himself now teaches at a war college in Georgia. If fortune had earlier dealt out a different hand, perhaps we would have visited Lee in the White House and seen Grant's property confiscated!

In the afternoon at 6:00, we traveled here by train and arrived at 11:30 p.m. Today is devoted to sightseeing in Philadelphia and tomorrow we go to New York, where I hope to receive your first letters. We left out

Baltimore to have more time for the North. The city is supposed to be unimportant; we traversed the length of the entire city by train and had a good look at it. The way from Washington to here passes through Baltimore, where the train is pulled from one station to the next by horses. Travel through the city takes about half an hour and proceeds right down the main streets. While we passed, many people hopped on the train to ride along for a little while and jumped off again when the engine was hooked on. What a bunch of heathens—but interesting!

Your good Prussian

Cataract House[40]
Niagara Falls, June 28, 1869

If the Niagara Falls were not so grandiose, I would have started this letter with a long description of our amusing stay in Philadelphia; another merry day in New York in the company of our best acquaintances (which especially now includes Rudolph's[41] friend Professor K.); our one-day excursion up the Hudson to Albany by steamboat (Uncle Alexander[42] will have to concede that a Rhine river journey is nothing compared to this); a pleasant evening in Albany; and finally, the train ride here, that took from 11:00 in the evening till 1:00 in the afternoon in a sleeping car. However, I am self-centered enough that I cannot stay away from this great natural spectacle for long. At the same time I long to describe it to you; that's why I leave all the other descriptions for the time I can give them to you in person. Just one thing I must mention first: I received all your longed-for letters, which luckily contained only good news. I was so anxious to hear from you that on arriving from Philadelphia I went directly to H. from the train station without going to the hotel first, dirty and dusty as I was; I had to apologize to him for my looks. Many thanks for everything you wrote. I was very pleased to hear how many people were interested in me and my arrival and ask you to thank them all. I would love to write a word to each, but I can't make time; with the exception of a small letter to Hugo[43] I have sent nothing that did not have your address; even the Horsleys, though I regret it deeply, were neglected and I am afraid it will stay this way. I can't help it—these four months must be used well.

The daily schedule of our trip since Wednesday the 23rd was the following: On the 24th, Philadelphia; on the 25th, from there to New York, arriving at noon; on the 26th at 7:00 a.m., up the Hudson, arriving in Albany at 4:00 p.m. On the same evening, departure, arriving here yesterday at noon on the 27th. What distances we are covering here! It does not look like much on a map, but still, for a trip like the one from New York to Richmond or to here, we would make elaborate preparations in Europe. But this is only a foretaste of what's to come. We will most likely change our travel plans significantly and depart tomorrow or the day after, whenever we can tear ourselves away from here, not to Chicago, but to Cincinnati, and on via Louisville to the Mammoth Caves, and then on to St. Louis. I have to disclose our "big idea" to you, our intention to visit California after all. Don't take fright but keep reading. Among all the people we have talked to, there are none who would not advise this; some even call it unreasonable to leave out such an opportunity while we are here. President Grant, to whom we mentioned this point, expressly assured us that it has been a long time since anything much has occurred with Indians in the areas we would cross; the Pacific Railway may be safer than the more frequented eastern lines; the climate in the part of California we are planning to visit, San Francisco and southeast of there, is reputed to be the best in the world. To be on the safe side we will not make our final decision till St. Louis, after we have gleaned more information from the locals. For this reason I asked Mr. von Krause for an introduction to the consul;[44] I also have one from B. and H., and Ernst has letters from another three prominent people. We will visit them all and find out whether they have heard anything disadvantageous. Grant also mentioned that several of the most prominent congressional delegates, Senator Sumner and others, as well as several delegates of foreign states, are presently taking a trip to California to make an official report on the condition of the train line. We promise that we will give up the project should we hear anything in St. Louis that does not agree with the reports so far. In that case we will leave St. Louis for Chicago, where we will add a leg up to Canada as planned earlier; if not, we will proceed to Omaha where the Pacific Railway starts. The trip from Omaha to San Francisco takes five days; we are likely to interrupt our trip in the middle for a six-day visit with the Mormons. Obviously the remainder of our time will then be devoted to California.

For the time being we have reached one of our main destinations. As I am writing this letter, I see the spray of the enormous waterfall: it extends upward from the abyss to far above the height from which the water is plunging down, the level at which our hotel is situated. This is the evening of our second day. Neither of us can make the decision to leave yet. I am curious how we will feel about it tomorrow or the day after. In addition to the falls' water columns and their colors that we cannot tire of watching, and the strange rumble which we cannot tire of hearing, there are many points of grandeur in the neighborhood of these falls which can barely be surveyed even superficially in two days.

The Niagara Falls are divided into two parts separated by Goat Island. The one belongs to America, the other to England, which means that one side is part of the United States, the other, of Canada. Our hotel is on the American side and looks over the American Falls. I have not managed to find out which side I would prefer since seeing each in turn makes one think that the one before you is the more beautiful. The American Falls are 800 feet wide and 164 feet high; the Canadian Falls (called Horseshoe Falls because of their form) are 2,000 feet wide and 156 feet high; the latter cataract has a place where it curves before falling. It is 22 feet deep and has an incredible emerald color. The rapids around Goat Island are an imposing sight (they drop off 51 feet in a stretch of 3,700 feet right before the river reaches the precipice). Equally imposing is the narrow area about two miles* below the falls where the water hurtles along between shores 300 feet high. In that place the entire river becomes a whirlpool, and it may sound incredible but the power of the water is so great that the middle of the river is 10 feet higher than the edges. This has been carefully measured. The most interesting of all we saw and experienced here was the Cave of Winds under a part of the American Falls called the Central Falls. This outing is quite dangerous and should only be undertaken by people without vertigo; the occasional lady has participated, but then these are American ladies.

I must describe this memorable tour. We began by visiting a specially prepared little house on Goat Island where we took off all our clothes and donned a double woolen waterproof costume, put leather caps on our heads, and wound some woolen rags around our feet. Dressed in this manner we followed our guide down a wooden spiral staircase to the foot of Goat Island, where the Horseshoe Falls plunges down on one side and the

---

* I hardly need to mention that I am referring to American miles in these letters. 75 American miles are 69 English ones.

American Falls on the other. In this place both the truly overwhelming magnificence of the spectacle as well as the massive water spray from both sides took our breath away. We stood there a while to recover our equilibrium. (It is only possible to communicate by signs. When I tried to shout something into the ear of our guide, I could not hear my own voice!) Then we proceeded in the direction of the American Falls. The rocks hurt our feet as we crossed the stream that had just passed Horseshoe Falls close to the rock wall of Goat Island. It is obvious that no other footwear but the woolen rags would be manageable here. We now reached the first big part of the American Falls which we had to cross. This Central Fall is 30 feet wide and the highest of the entire Niagara Falls. At this point, the rock wall of Goat Island forms a small, shallow grotto. It is called Cave of Winds because the enormous mass of the water creates a draft of air that violently squeezes into it. The main part of the Central Falls precipitates itself in front of this cave, but sufficient water penetrates part of the cave still. On with it!

It is impossible to describe the impression that followed. We were like Tamino passing through fire and water. The stunning air pressure, the masses of water that fell on our heads and bathed face and body, the enormous power of the water that was making for the bottom from a height of 160 feet and plunging right past our heads; all this has to be experienced! According to everyone who has gone through the experience, it is a foretaste of drowning. We walked through the fall on a wooden board with a railing on one side that helped us pull ourselves along when we had to close our eyes because of the horrible power of the elements; it is not helpful to look downward either because the water sprays upward with a vehemence similar to that from above. The worst place is a little past the middle point. I am told that many people cannot pass this point and turn around instead. We managed to continue and reached the other side of the Central Falls comfortably, landing between it and the rest of the American Falls where we were only sprayed by mist, no longer by the actual stream of water. We rested for a few moments before returning by climbing around the falls. This last half is harder and more exhausting but we did not feel that we were choking as much. The danger of being pulled along by the churning water, that at this point shoots along horizontally, was great for we had to balance on rocks without any path or boards. Again the woolen rags on our feet helped because they literally clung to the rock.

When we had mounted the stairs again we both sang "Greetings to thee, oh sunlight"[45] and dried ourselves off thoroughly. Lightheadedness was not absent. We received a certificate that we had managed to complete the difficult path. I am enclosing mine for your amusement. Please keep it till I am back.

We undertook another excursion on the Canadian side of Table Rock that was not half as dangerous. There it was enough to pull a waterproof garment over our clothes. This provided for, we watched the first part of Horseshoe Falls hurtle past us. Since we had the opportunity, we had our picture taken on the Canadian shore in our waterproof costume with the real Niagara Falls as background. These pictures will be a special remembrance for us, and they turned out to be good likenesses. We sat for the photographer before we went down to Horseshoe Falls and received the finished pictures in a frame when we came back out.

What all I could write about still! But it is late and I must go to bed. I need to mention that I had a visit from a certain Mr. Wilcox from Peoria,[46] Illinois, last night. He lives in the same hotel and wanted to see me because of my name. He said his wife's greatest wish was to meet a relative of Uncle Felix; I let him introduce us and spent a few pleasant hours talking to her. The couple is on their honeymoon trip; they invited Ernst and me to visit them and stay with them. Maybe we will do that. It was astonishing how much the young lady knew about our family even though she has never left America; she asked whether my father's name was Paul[47] and whether Sebastian,[48] Hensel's[49] only son, was still alive, etc. This familiarity cheered me in such a remote place!

I wanted to tell you that I force myself not to get up before 8 a.m. while I am here, to avoid the v. d. Heydt danger[50] of getting engaged at 5:00 a.m. The opportunities for this are plentiful, should one choose. There are many pretty, young girls around, along with many honeymooning couples who serve as stimulating examples.

Ernst thanks you for the greetings and returns them all.

Blondin (but *under* the Niagara Falls)[51]

P.S. I can't quite forgo talking about Philadelphia. Aside from two hours in the State Penitentiary, the model of "Pennsylvanian solitary confinement," I found Girard College[52] (named after its founder) worth mentioning and very strange. This is an institution for orphaned children of both sexes and seems to me the most splendid charitable foundation I have experienced. Over an extensive area containing big playgrounds and athletic fields, there are no less than five big buildings of white marble, two of which are used for teaching purposes and built in the Classical style, like the temple at Paestum.[53] The founder, Girard, decided on the statutes: they forbid any religious functionary from entering the grounds. I am quoting him below so that you understand his reasons. They have left me impressed.

Extract from the Will of Stephen Girard
[in English in the original]

There are, however, some restrictions, which I consider it my duty to prescribe, and to be, amongst others, conditions on which my bequest for said College is made, and to be enjoyed, namely ... Secondly, I enjoin and require that no ecclesiastic, missionary, or minister of any sect whatsoever, shall ever hold or exercise any station or duty whatever in the said College; nor shall any such person ever be admitted for any purpose, or as a visitor, within the premises appropriated to the purposes of the said college:—In making this restriction, I do not mean to cast any reflection upon any sect or person whatsoever; but, as there is such a multitude of sects, and such a diversity of opinion amongst them, I desire to keep the tender minds of the orphans, who are to derive advantage from this bequest, free from the excitement which clashing doctrines and sectarian controversy are so apt to produce; my desire is, that all the instructors and teachers in the College, shall take pains to instill into the minds of the scholars, the purest principles of morality, so that, on their entrance into active life, they may from inclination and habit, evince benevolence toward their fellow creatures, and a love of truth, sobriety and industry, adopting at the same time such religious tenets as their matured reason may enable them to prefer.

St. Nicholas Hotel
Cincinnati (Ohio), July 3, 1869

Today you get the agreed-upon sign of life, dear parents, to tell you that we are both in splendid form, as always, but time is too short to send longer letters. The mail is about to go out, and if I wait till the next time, the gap between communications will be too long.

In short, we left Niagara Falls on Tuesday and arrived here the next morning after 21 hours on the train, with a two-hour break in Buffalo that gave us time to look around the city. We had meant to go on tomorrow toward Louisville and the Mammoth Cave, but there is no direct train on Sundays, so we preferred to extend our sojourn here. Cincinnati is a city that can be enjoyed for a few days of comfortable leisure. The surroundings offer attractive rides, and the suburbs, especially Clifton, which is situated on a hill and rich in pretty views, contain such tasteful parks and private villas as I have not found anywhere in the New World other than in New York. In Cincinnati, Germans are the most numerous element. Would that be the reason?

Yesterday we experienced a tropical thunderstorm; I had never been exposed to lightning and thunder following each other so relentlessly, accompanied by torrential rains. Not that it relieved the great heat we have been enduring the last few days.

Southern Hotel[54]
St. Louis (Missouri), July 8, 1869

Dear parents, I hope you received my second-to-last letter and will not be surprised if I say today: off to California! We arrived here yesterday morning and made the visits we had planned. Since well-informed people confirm all previous reports of the Pacific Railroad, we have now decided to travel away from you by the same distance again as that which separates us already at this point. To see such a vast part of the world will be a broadening experience indeed! How many new and interesting things and conditions we will encounter beyond the Rocky Mountains and the prairies, not to mention our visit with the Mormons!

The main reason we wish to head farther and farther west is that America seems stranger and more remarkable the farther we travel from the eastern parts. This will not be a pleasure trip, strictly speaking. No theater, no promenades, no comfortable carriages, not even *great* natural beauty. Watching culture as it moves forward from the East, step by step, sending out the pioneers of civilization westward—that can really be called an adventure.

Beside the casual conversations on trains, steamers, and roads, we find that the long exchanges with people to whom we had introductions in the various cities teach us much and give us a picture of this fabulous country, of the incredible riches still unexplored, the yet-to-be exploited resources, the rapid creation and growth of cities, and the only ambition of its inhabitants: making money. Everyone will do what it takes to bring in money. They are not ashamed if they can save and they want to earn. The educated person works with the intention of amassing a fortune as fast as possible and then taking off. Where to? He does not know yet but possibly to a place where he won't see groups of haggling men, where he will hear something other than "making money," where he can encounter a full life of the mind, where people have ways and means of making their lives more beautiful and pleasant, where there is not just the naked prose of life without art and higher culture. I have to admit I would find a stay in any of the American cities of the West for any length of time or forever quite horrible and practically impossible. The reasons also include the republican constitution to which I have more aversion the more I experience its effects. I already had this reaction to it from my reading and here, I mistrust the communist tendencies which are of course more evident in a republic than in a monarchy.

I can tolerate the political equality of all classes, but flirting with social equality is insupportable, since only dreamers can believe in it. For an everyday example, take traveling by train, which is supposedly without any distinction of class. It may not be very important, but it is interesting to look at the causes for this attempt at equality and the enthusiasm with which it is justified by members of a certain party. There is supposed to be no preferment: The rich are kept from paying a few dollars more so they can avoid being in contact with their dirty and drunken brethren for several days; the educated man is supposed to take his place next to rough-and-tumble chaps. He is not allowed into the carriage which is reserved for ladies or gentlemen accompanying ladies, because justifiably so, the rough chap is not allowed either.

Will we be able to prevent the same people who were forced to keep bad company while on the train from going to a costly hotel as soon as they turn their back to the train and by that very action restore the barrier? Can we keep them from hiring a carriage to be shown around while their "friends" from the train have to travel the muddy street in torn shoes? In addition to the inconveniences which such customs entail for the better classes, the motives will create even greater damage, fostering incorrect ideas in the heads of the lower classes (I dare use this distinction even though I am in America).

If I remember correctly, I have already mentioned how lazy and useless the servants generally are. Only the blacks show the occasional will to work. I will therefore not elaborate further today. Here, at the beginning of what is called "the West," one has to battle another problem: the high wages. The wage of a maid starts at $120 and up; this low rate is only for the most common people. Male servants are hard to come by except in hotels and rare anyway, because they can find plenty of opportunity to work for themselves. It becomes a luxury to keep servants, which many of the educated but not rich cannot afford. They are forced to do as much as possible themselves. Mr. O., with whom I talked here, himself carries the water to the kitchen where his wife does the cooking; he splits the wood and cleans the street in front of his house. He has no reason to feel self-conscious, since there is no choice. When he was selling a sewing machine the other day, he put it on his shoulder and carried it through the city. He would have had to pay a carrier an immense sum. He did not feel ashamed of this either because any friend seeing him would not have minded, other than counting how much money he is likely to save by carrying it himself!

Mr. R, head of F.A.R. and Co., where H. sent me and with whom I spent last evening at the German Club, talked to me about how much trouble he has finding workers. A common worker in his flour mill earns $3–4 per day for light work. If he needs someone for harder work (being exposed to the sun or "other difficulties"), he can offer $10 without finding anyone. A "gentleman" would rather take $3–4 and work in the shade.

Enough for today about the conditions here. I don't really want to describe too many details since I don't have the time to study everything more carefully in these four months. But you will appreciate a passing word about such matters.

It is strange how fascinating the daily life is. I seem to be unable to give as thorough a description of our trip as I did last year on my travels through Scotland. In addition, a general restlessness makes me want to inspect and listen to the street rather than taking the leisure to write long letters. Admittedly I don't resist this temptation and so I feel justified in using the opportunity provided by the time I saved.

One of the most famous personalities in America is the senator and general Karl Schurz (liberator of the poet Gottfried Kinkel) whom we visited yesterday. Karl Schurz is a big name even though he is relatively young, about in his midforties. One climbs to his office in the business building of the *Western Post*[55] (the newspaper of which he is co-owner and co-editor) on two wobbly wooden staircases such as you would find in a hayloft. Many people waiting and papers all over the place are to be expected in the office of a journalist. His personality is little like a Bolz in the comedy by Freytag.[56] He is a calm, gentle man. I can't say whether he only seems that way because of a slight malaise he's suffering from at present. We visited him again today at his house and were received in a friendly manner both times. At our request, he wrote us an introduction to the Mormon delegate to Congress, Captain Hooper. As an aside I note that many workmen were busy at his house when we arrived there today. When we asked whether the pretty new-looking house was being reno-vated we were told that this was not the case. The front of the house had subsided several inches during the night before and needed to be repaired. Inside everything was as usual.

It is hard to describe how I feel, now that I'm at the Mississippi River. When we passed its western bank yesterday, coming from Indianapolis, I remembered all kinds of stories and descriptions of the "Father of Waters" that we had read as children. I could not fathom that I was there and that all the huge steamboats, the "Mississippi Steamers," were heading for New Orleans. As in the harbor of New York, a big ferry awaits the passengers from the train, who are then carried up at a gallop by five or six carriages with four-horse teams. The ferry takes them across the river, which is about a mile wide at this point. The water looks yellow and muddy and the banks are very low. The enormous rainstorms which have yet to stop have made the wild Missouri river even wilder, and it carries all its dirt into the Mississippi, which is supposedly completely clear above their confluence. The water pipes in St. Louis are affected by this and the washing water in our hotel leaves a rim of dirt as soon as it stands for a few minutes. "It is clean water nevertheless," as a hotel servant assured us. The hotel is first class by the way and we have rooms with private baths, etc.

Before I talk more about St. Louis, I want to briefly describe our trip here. We left Cincinnati on Monday afternoon, traveling by boat because the train track had become blocked that morning by the collapse of a bridge with a freight train on it. The trip on the Ohio was splendid and we were happy that we had not missed it. There were pretty views of the wooded and sparsely settled banks, and the great heat was softened pleasantly by the breeze of the boat's motion. We sat peacefully on deck for 10 hours and drank in nature till we arrived at Louisville in the evening. The only thing bothering us was the terrible spitting around us. This seems to be worse here than elsewhere. It happened across my head, arms and legs, always admittedly with great accuracy, but I barely dared to move for fear of being hit if I did. The deck was soon so dirty that I hung my legs across the railing to keep my boots clean.

I must mention another American custom, not quite as bad but bound to get the attention of the European traveler on most ships, regarding the common meals included in the ticket price. As soon as the black servant rings the bell as a sign that the meal is on the table, the entire crowd runs for the dining hall and looks for places to sit. If you are not quick it can happen that you won't find a seat because the tickets are passed out on demand while the places at the tables are limited. This hurry does not stop during the meal; nobody speaks and everyone is busy gulping down as much and as fast as possible, using fingers as needed. I don't know why this haste. I suspect it is so they can return to their favorite occupation: the spitting, something they stop during the meal with surprising tact, maybe in consideration of the ladies who all take the head end of the tables with their gentlemen, but only with theirs. The meals are the same morning, noon, and night, except that tea and coffee are replaced by soup for lunch and the latter is supplemented with vegetables like cabbage or squash. Eggs, salt fish, omelets, chops, beefsteaks, ham, and a thousand other dishes are the regular fare; each dish is presented in a separate bowl so there are legions of them on the table. One bowl unfortunately tastes the same as the other. Hot rolls are the bread Americans eat with passion, which makes them all dyspeptic. It's quite difficult to get cold bread. It is altogether replaced by hot bread on the breakfast table.

In Louisville we stayed in a grandiose hotel, the Galt House,[57] and took the train the next morning for four hours and an open carriage for three (the last of which tossed us about more than the *Scotia* in a storm) to get to the Mammoth Cave. This is an underground cave whose dimensions are not yet known. A hike of 18 miles is the usual trip, which is likely only a small part of the cave; the bigger part has yet to be explored. We limited our trip to 9 miles in a group of 12 people, each with a hanging lamp. The many passages and grottos house a few impressive stalactites and rock formations which we wandered through, some narrow enough that we could not remain upright, others so high that we could hardly make out the ceiling. Once we forced our way through a narrow passage called "fat man's misery" because someone corpulent would not fit through; then we reached a big grotto called the Star Chamber because the ceiling looks like the night sky once the lights are dimmed and only a faint gleam falls on the upper wall—an impressive illusion. We saw many strange things one after another.

The most spectacular feature is clearly the vastness of this cave. The temperature inside is the same summer and winter. Just at the entrance, where warm air leaves the cave in the winter and gets pushed into it in the summer, one feels a draft that can be so strong in certain weather conditions that it will extinguish a light. About 200 feet from the entrance is a little hut which was used by consumptives hoping for healing in the unchanging temperature. They were supplied with nourishment every day from the outside. As far as I have heard, this did not help the healing process and the solitaries were not spared an early death. Maybe the lack of sunlight canceled out the good influence of the even temperature.

The cave has several ponds in which swim—wonderful to see—live fish and crabs *without eyes*. Nature seems to have left those out in these creatures because they don't need them in the complete darkness of their environment. I am bringing along a fish and a crab preserved in alcohol to show you this strange fact. The fish is about 3½ inches long, white and so transparent that one can see every fiber in its body. The next morning we left the rather awful inn near the cave and went back to Louisville, took a ferry across the Ohio to the suburb of Jeffersonville on the right bank of the river and from there the train to here without a stop. We arrived the next day at 8:00 in the morning after a 25-hour trip. In Indianapolis, a sleeping car was provided which we used with exceptional success.

Tomorrow, should it please the gods, we will start on our long trip. First, 26 hours to Omaha. We might stay there overnight or continue right away on the Union Pacific Railway, which links up with the Central Pacific Railway in Salt Lake. Omaha to Salt Lake City, the capital of the Mormons, will take two more days and nights on the train and about 30 miles in a carriage; Salt Lake City is not directly on the train line. From Salt Lake City to San Francisco via Sacramento will again take two days and nights.

I will write again from Salt Lake City; however, the letter might take a long time to get to you. Don't be concerned if you have no news for longer than usual. The postal service is rather slipshod and a letter may easily get lost going halfway around the world!

P.S. The north German consul[58] we had introductions to, from B. and from Washington, was very friendly to us. He visited us yesterday at the hotel for two hours and later picked us up to be introduced to his family, consisting of a wife and an amiable daughter. We spent a pleasant evening there. I must mention that they showed us, among other things, a vase from the Royal Prussian Porcelain Factory, the king's present to the consul, and an album of photographs from the Dresden Gallery—both rare objects in this place!

Today we were introduced to the entire journalistic staff of the *Western Post* and invited for several bottles of wine by the editors, sharing them with many people from different classes and nations invited in our honor. The number of Germans in St. Louis is relatively larger than in any other city. Of 230,000 inhabitants, more than 100,000 are German. It is amazing to think that only 5,000 people lived in St. Louis in 1830.

Metropolitan Hotel[59]
Omaha City (Nebraska), July 11, 1869

By one, or rather several, coincidences, I have time, dear parents, to send you another cheerful good-bye before I start the trip across the vast ocean of land. We expected to arrive here yesterday afternoon and to leave this morning on the Pacific Railway. Instead, we did not arrive till this afternoon and won't be able to go on board till tomorrow morning. This is how it happened: The two Missouri trains that travel here (the Hannibal–St. Joseph line, as well as the St. Joseph–Council Bluffs line, whose memory may now be guaranteed forever by my account) cannot deal with the great masses of rain we have had. So first we had to stay in a miserable hole by the name of Hamilton for five hours because half of a bridge had been swept away. Once it was fixed, more or less, we encountered long stretches of rail (one, for instance, was four miles long) that were flooded by the Missouri. The train could not drive any faster than a common horse-drawn carriage. So instead of 24 hours, the trip to Omaha took 40 hours and we missed our connection. Just like pious Englishmen, we are now spending our Sunday quietly in Omaha. It comes at a useful moment and can be relished. I am using the noonday hour to write this letter because it is too hot to be outside. Toward evening we plan to stroll into the city, whose situation on the Missouri is very pretty.

It is rather pleasant that the nights are cool and refreshing so that we can sleep well and we are both in good shape and health. We are well equipped for our trip, the main thing being a big basket full of pâtés, sausages, crackers, red wine, cognac, etc. with napkins, knives and forks, and cups. We bought all of these supplies, sweating in the unforgettable heat of St. Louis, running from one shop to the next. There will be eating houses on the way for meals, but it can always happen that we are stuck somewhere and have to wait for a while. So this caution, common to all travelers, is well worth it. By the way, we were greatly tempted on the way here to break into the supplies already because there were no meals, since it's not usually necessary to count on them, but we restrained ourselves and starved so we could dedicate the provisions to the Pacific Railway trip. We already have our tickets to San Francisco; we reserved two beds in the "Pullman's Palace Sleeping Car" (two of which accompany each express train). Our carriage goes through all the way to the salt lake.

To highlight certain American circumstances for you, here is the following: Having heard various rumors from other passengers about the haphazard train conditions, I asked the conductor (as usual a corpulent black fellow) when I entered the sleeping car on the Missouri train: "Well, how is the road?" His cool answer: "Rather bad, Sir!" If we tried to ask such a question between Berlin and Cologne we would get a different response!

It is so full here that we did not find rooms at the hotel we had meant to stay in. A lot of people pass through on their way West, fewer the other way around. Omaha will surely grow significantly in a short time with this increased traffic. In the brief months since the world has heard anything about these few wooden houses, the number of inhabitants has grown to 18,000.

Townsend House[60]
Salt Lake City (Utah), July 15, 1869

Despite my past ridicule of certain philosophers who claim that nothing is real, including their own person, I am rather tempted now to become their follower. I had never had the least idea that I would be able to visit the city of the Mormons and I can hardly take in the reality of it, now that I am here! When I imagine that I arrived here via the greatest and most wonderful product of human endeavors that has evolved in the last few years and that I have witnessed half of the extent of the Pacific Railway, it is all the more reason not to feel real. I will either have to write a whole book about this trip or just allude to it in short general remarks.

I must mention that Ernst and I are planning—should we not change our mind—to send a report on the Pacific Railway from San Francisco to one of the great newspapers in Berlin, maybe the *National-Zeitung*. In St. Louis the editors of the *Western Post* begged us to send them such a report. We will probably not do so. Such an article has to be written with care and must therefore have attention, which would take time and which we would perhaps sacrifice to our people in Berlin but not necessarily to those in St. Louis, to whom we have a distant relationship only. As I said, we will think this through once more. Truth-loving American journalists must be interested in getting impartial if lay reports about this great achievement. This can only be surmised when one sees how often even official reporters are subject to corruption and party passions.

Now to our trip. We left Omaha City Monday, July 12, at 8:30 a.m. and arrived in Uintah, the station where we left the train, on Wednesday at 10:30 in the morning, more or less on time. Our train was not very long: locomotive, two luggage and three passenger cars, and two sleeping cars at the end. The passenger cars were fairly empty, but the sleeping cars quite full of Californians, among them a young widow with her brother whom we had met in St. Louis and with whom we have formed a "friendship for life." When we separated yesterday because they went straight on to San Francisco, we had already made plans to meet again. We shared our breakfast baskets freely and traded refreshments of all kinds.

The other people traveling with us, with whom we had a relationship like one on a long sea voyage, were much more decent and had better manners than we encountered on any other train trip in America. A young French engineer, Mr. Jozon,[61] whom we met in Omaha, is a pleasant companion who helps me practice the French that has rather retreated in favor of English, as I noticed to my horror. Like us, he is traveling to see the world.

In the first 500 miles from Omaha, the train crosses prairies, endless as an ocean, with that strange long grass that makes waves in the wind like the water in the sea. I notice that the grass in the prairies we crossed on the Missouri train was higher yet, often as tall as a man. Don't think that they are even in elevation; the horizon is interrupted by different ground levels; only the vegetation stays the same, as far as the eye can see. Occasionally one sees small rural inns and block houses surrounded by fields with high cornstalks and oats, and free-range cattle and horses. On this trip we often see Indian wigwams whose inhabitants seem to belong to friendly tribes. I met the first Indians in Omaha, where they were shooting arrows at a target. They seemed tame and a little degenerate for somebody looking at them from Cooper's point of view. I could not distinguish the faces of the ones we passed along our way. I will mention more about these gentlemen at the end of this letter.

The first 500 miles are in a straight line and one has the impression that there is no rise at all. In fact, we were climbing about 10 feet per mile. When we woke up in Cheyenne the next morning, at the end of this stretch we had arrived at 5,931 feet. I discovered this in a strange way. When I got up (does that not sound funny: getting up in a train?) and looked at my barometer, I saw that it pointed to 22.9″. In the morning it had shown 28.6″. I thought it was surely broken till I remembered that we had changed elevation by 5,000 feet (Omaha is 966 feet above sea level).

The so-called train "stations" consist of one or maybe two or three houses; they supply the locomotive with the necessary wood and water; we arrive at the eating houses I told you about three times a day. The train stops at each one for about half an hour so the passengers can be fed. The meals were good at the start but were getting worse closer to the middle of the stretch. This is understandable because hardly anything grows in this area and everything has to be transported from far away. Among the strange meals we were served, I must mention antelope steak. Antelopes run in big herds and are a pretty sight when they flee, shied away by the noise of the train or the crack of a shotgun that a fellow traveler will push out of the window for fun.

The eating houses are usually in settled places that may well develop into cities in the future. Now they are a conglomeration of block houses. The names of these "cities" are Grand Island, North Platte, Cheyenne, Laramie, Rawlings, Wahsatch; Grand Island has 400, Cheyenne 3,800, and Laramie 1,000 inhabitants. Keeping in mind that I am still talking about the first 500 miles of our trip, on average we saw a log cabin every 12 to 15 miles and an eating house every 75 to 100 miles. Small and larger military detachments, protection against unfriendly Indians, bivouac about every 20 miles, partly in the stations, partly in tents.

The higher we climb the better and more agreeable the air becomes. As usual in the mountains the sun burns, but in the shade it is very pleasant and the nights are cool enough that one can make use of the woolen blankets in the sleeping cars. The beauty of the sunsets in this part of America is so famous that I need only refer to it as an aside. Throughout the entire trip they provided us with much enjoyment. The first sight of the prairie was rich in colorful displays. When complete darkness had descended, there was a show of lightning which set the entire horizon afire as I had not seen it before.

The next stop, the morning after leaving Omaha, was Cheyenne, where we saw the snowy Rocky Mountains for the first time. From there it is about two hours to the highest point of the Pacific Railway, a station by the name of Sherman. It is 8,342 feet above sea level; European locomotives have yet to reach such an elevation. From Cheyenne to Sherman we climbed another 2,300 feet; for this stretch the train was pulled by two locomotives. The elevation gain per mile was 88.176 feet.

Until the next morning, we stayed at about the same elevation, about 7,000 feet, more or less. The barometer showed 21.5″ in Sherman, the lowest reading I have observed. The air was getting better and better. We enjoyed the relief from the eastern heat. In the evening we would sit on the platform of our sleeping car in coats.

About half an hour after Cheyenne the lush prairie grass stops; you see bare hills and strange sandstone formations here and there; sometimes we crossed a deep canyon or small river on a fairly flat plain. These plains are made of red granite; occasionally the train cuts through rock of this color. We approached the snowy mountains, which go up to 17,000 feet (higher than the Alps), but stayed at a certain distance from them. The train traveled about 150 miles in this manner. The lighting and colors of the mountains were beautiful beyond words. The following 150 miles led us through a desert: no trees, no grass—just what one would imagine a desert to be. Here the workers building the tracks have to be supplied with water by special trains because the water in the occasional little puddles in the sandy ditches and small lakes we passed is bitter and salty. Where some of these ditches are dried up you see a white substance, the salt residue. The edges of the lakes are also covered with this substance. In these last 150 miles we crossed the watershed at an elevation of 7,000 feet. From here the water flows to the east toward the Atlantic and to the West toward the Pacific.

The Green River is a boundary of this part of the landscape. Here we found traces of green and more vegetation. Certain formations of the terrain are unusual: long, wide openings, frequently like beds of dried-out rivers or artificially constructed paths or buildings. It is astonishing how regularly such formations appear; they seem as if formed by human hands. Grotesque rock masses that look like churches or people are everywhere and surprise us as they suddenly appear. It is as if we had escaped the desolation and were in a city again.

Now we arrived at the last part of our trip between Wahsatch and Uintah. Wahsatch is still 6,819 feet high; from there, in 3½ hours, the train descends about 2,500 feet on the western slope of the Rocky Mountains. This was the most difficult engineering feat. We traveled in big curves, through tunnels, long rocky crevasses, and endless bridges and viaducts through deep valleys. Sometimes we climbed steeply once more for a few hundred feet. The path was highly interesting. The view was limited because the train wound through narrow valleys enclosed by immensely high granite and sandstone rocks. These valleys are referred to by the Spanish word *canyon*. The largest ones are the Echo and Weber Canyons. Through these, we reached the plateau of the Salt Lake. There are already Mormons living in the canyons; we could see the occasional farmhouse belonging to this sect on the banks of small mountain creeks.

Uintah is still on the Pacific Railway, or Railroad as the Americans say, which goes all the way to Promontory. That's where the Central Pacific Railway starts. I can, however, conclude the description of the Union Pacific Railway now because the distance to Promontory from here is only about 60 miles. A description of the Central Pacific Railway will follow from San Francisco! As a layman I cannot judge the train construction, but these facts are obvious to everyone: The trains run on a single track (like all the American trains except for a few in the East). The bridges are always made of wood; the embankment is generally so narrow that the cars extend beyond them on both sides, the crevices so narrow that one must be careful not to stretch a hand out the window. Sometimes there is a rock overhang, making an imminent collapse possible. Most of the deficient points are being worked on, especially the substitution of iron bridges for the wooden ones. At especially insecure spots they station a guard—a post that seems to me worse than being the keeper of the Eddystone light.[62] Even he is less isolated from the world!

The most dangerous thing is the superficial way in which the rails are assembled and fastened. Despite all this, supposedly no bad accident has occurred yet. That would be more than one can say of any American rail line which has existed for more than a few months. Generally the trains proceed slowly, reasonably, and with caution. Still, the last carriage on our train derailed twice within one hour, but without injury to anyone. Communication with the locomotive is excellent; the derailment was reported immediately and the train stopped. It was especially easy in our case because one accident was on a bridge and the other on a viaduct where the locomotive had stopped its engine already anyway. For us this fact was less than reassuring because it is better not to stay on those bridges longer than necessary. By the way, the braking mechanism as well as the machines helping to heave the carriage back onto the tracks are highly practical and ingenious. All in all, I can't say that this train is worse than any other in America. However, we can't apply our European security standards. They say that the Central Pacific Railway tops the Union Pacific. I will report on that honestly when the time comes.

When we left the train in Uintah we encountered two four-in-hand coaches which took us travelers to Salt Lake City. The distance is 25 miles and it took us five hours. The route was an unending succession of irregular elevations and dips; we were rattled around as if our bones must break. The road proceeded through a waterless, sandy desert, no grass, only gnarled bushes, along barren mountains; suddenly when we had reached the top of the incline we saw the deep-blue lake in front of us, much bluer than Lake

Geneva or the Italian lakes—an indescribable experience. The view now stayed spectacular so that we wished that the otherwise very uncomfortable trip would never end. On the other side of the lake at a distance of many miles, we saw a long chain of high, rocky mountains, to the south the snow-covered Wahsatch mountains at whose base lies Salt Lake City. Here the often-mentioned color display seemed the most extraordinary. In *the middle of the day* we could see blue, violet, pink, and a heavenly smell enveloped the air, as in a fairy tale. Such a great contrast between the dead desert in our immediate surroundings and this view! It was easy to picture the other side as a fairyland. The effect is entirely due to the colors. The other side is no less desert than this.

I can't write much about Salt Lake City because I have not yet looked around sufficiently. I am hoping that I will be able to write you another letter from here with a description of the Mormons. If not, I will write from San Francisco. Today I just want to tell you that the entire city is a real miracle, even at the first superficial glance. It is spread out in the middle of the desert sands, about 15 miles from the lake. The broadly built streets are planted with lawns and trees; small creeks bringing drinking water from the mountains, artificially guided by small dams, pleasantly refresh the air. It looks like a village, with small clean houses that are pretty and appetizing. Our hotel, Townsend House, is built like the others and very rural, rather fit for a long stay. We are decided to stay here at least for four days so we can attend the Sunday service at the Tabernacle and refresh ourselves with the splendid air up here—we are probably about 4,500 feet high. It is warm, but a cooling wind keeps blowing from the lake. Yesterday evening it was already magnificent after 6:00 p.m. It feels like a genuine Swiss atmosphere. My barometer shows 24″ today.

We have seen two strange things since arriving here: a performance in the theater which belongs to Brigham Young, who is known to be the head of the Mormon sect, and a camp of three Indian tribes. We attended two comedies last night in the spacious, handsome theater, which is a little bigger than our *Schauspielhaus*, quite well equipped with good decorations and costumes. The plays were performed moderately well; the prima donna was an adorable actress from California, advertised simply as Lotta, who is living in our hotel. She delights us with her appearance at meals. The audience furnishings are simple; the seats, except in the front rows and the orchestra boxes, are made of wood; the kerosene lighting is sparse. The orchestra of 20 men played some of the dances quite well. The most interesting was the audience, in which the women were by far in the majority. As we heard, the Mormons tend to go out with *one* wife only, but they seem to make an exception for the theater. We saw some with 2, 3, or 5 women and several children; when we went for an ice cream afterward a lot of men came in, each with several women. They all sat quietly to themselves. Nobody joined another group. In general the seriousness and calm of these people is striking; each of them behaves with gravity, not much like the Americans in general. More of that later when I have learned more about my Mormons.

Now a few words about the other strange thing—the savages. Until recently there were frequent bloody skirmishes and even more secret murders pitting Mormons against Indians in this part of the desert and prairies. A while ago, Brigham Young undertook personal visits to a number of tribes that were not too hostile and made contracts with them that seem to be largely honored. Every three weeks or so, individual tribes come to Salt Lake City for a few days to renew those contracts, to trade goods, and buy supplies. For this purpose Brigham Young has had a special building erected with barns for the horses and a large courtyard in which the Indians camp. The day before yesterday, three tribes arrived: the Snakes, Shoshones and Goshutes. The appearance of the courtyard tops anything I have ever seen. It is square. In the middle and at several other spots, they light large bonfires to roast meat and warm milk that they stir with little sticks of wood. Some of them crouch around the fires on their knees, others lounge along the walls of the yard. The chieftain of the tribes is an old man whose face is not unintelligent and who reminds me a bit of Cooper's Chingachook. He was reclining on a mattress with indescribable grandeur; he is the only one who knows a few words of English. They are all copper red; many have painted their faces with cinnabar and look hideous. You know from much I have experienced willingly that I am not a coward. But when I was standing in the middle of this yard with Ernst and the Frenchman, surrounded by hundreds of those savages, I can't deny that my heart raced a bit for a few minutes. Those fellows are personified wildness, looking at us with the expression of animals, and they don't change their look when we smile at them. All three of us surmised that should we confront them in the desert by ourselves, our scalps might not stay on our heads for long. They have the fixed stare peculiar to the mad and the savage and they are covered with dirt. It was impossible to distinguish men from women when they were completely dressed, which was hardly the case for the majority. They wear buffalo hides and colorful shawls given to them by the inhabitants here. The hair is the same length for both sexes. It hangs down or is sometimes worn in a braid. Almost all the women wear clasps, beads, and coins on their arms and necks. One of them pulls along two stolen white children who have become half Indians; I pity those poor things, whose origin is hard to hide no matter how they try to conceal it. The barns hold 150–180 horses on which they ride by twos and threes. When they ride or walk, the women carry the infants in a basket on their back, tightly wrapped in fur, which keeps the little ones stiffly upright. I saw a boy of 4 or 5 years who was sucking his mother's breast comfortably, standing on the ground next to the sitting woman. I spent 1½ hours in the yard and inspected everything carefully, once the really unpleasant first impression had passed. I can hardly find words to describe the untamed savagery and wickedness which was visible in the eyes of most of those Indians. Even their language is like the grunts and squeaks of animals. When I saw them sitting around their fires with long knives in their hands, stirring their kettles, laughing wildly, talking to each other with lively gestures, I was grateful that there are 20,000 Mormons here in addition to us. The dogs that accompany them are half wolves; like them, they sleep with pricked ears. In short, just as Anatole says everything is old, so I say everything is wild.

I feel strange when my thoughts cross over to you in the serene landscape of Switzerland, where I presume you will be by the time this letter arrives, while I am in a desert among polygamists, living close to wild Indian tribes. We are certainly in very different situations; strange for such a harmonious family! But I know this much: this trip is the sunniest time of my life and I am forever in great spirits—don't laugh at me!—like someone who has half-finished a task and is anxious to complete it.

Salt Lake City, July 18, 1869
Together with my previous letter I enclose the local paper, the *Deseret Evening News*, where you can find us under "Arrivals" on the second page.

You will have to admit that we are making good use of our trip when I tell you that we went to visit Brigham Young the day before yesterday and had a short talk with him. The previous day we looked up our Mormon, the congressional delegate Captain W. Hooper, and handed him the introduction from General Schurz. It seems to have been to our advantage, as we anticipated. We did not find Hooper in, but he came to look us up two hours later and promised to check with Brigham right away whether he could receive us. The next morning he picked us up at 10 o'clock to take us to the President. On the way there he introduced us to everyone we encountered with the remark: two gentlemen from Europe. According to the American principle of equality, we became used to greeting and shaking hands with merchants, day laborers, judges, bakers, and carriage drivers, all mixed together. Hooper had asked me whether I was related to the "great Mendelssohn" and then never omitted adding to my name: nephew of the great composer. Ernst was rather amused that this repeated itself at least 50 times. You will be pleased to hear that Uncle is known and appreciated even here; more even among the women, since the men have interests other than the arts. The way in which I heard him mentioned in this foreign part of the world has given me many moments of pleasure. The expression "world renowned" is not just a phrase in his case.

The Mormons we met on our walk to the President seemed partly quite pleasant and educated people. Many have been missionaries in Europe; even the owner of our hotel has preached in England, and the editor and owner of the *Deseret News* functioned as an apostle in Germany. The postmaster (a gentile—that is, not a Mormon), with whom we spend a lot of time, teaches us many useful and interesting facts about the city and its inhabitants, also about issues which one is not allowed to bring up with the Mormons, especially the subject of polygamy or in the descriptive wording of their doctrine the "spiritual wife system." The Mormons will not talk about this with a stranger, fearing either undue curiosity, mockery, or contempt. In his position as an employee of the USA, the postmaster has access to and insight into everything. As an educated man, he is equipped to convey a concept correctly.

Salt Lake City presently has about 20,000 inhabitants. The entire state of Utah has about 150,000. About 99 percent of these are Mormons, almost all polygamists. Hooper is one of the few exceptions and is satisfied with one wife. Brigham Young has a lot, nobody knows the exact number; the average for all Mormons is supposedly 3–4. The wives take the name of the man and are addressed by their first name to be told apart or add their previous name to that of their husband.

The blossoming and thriving of this desert city is miraculous, as is the organization which was imparted and given life by Brigham Young, the heart and blood of this community. Church and religion—as with all new sects the object of the fanaticism of its members—are completely controlled by him, and this fanaticism creates a kind of blind obedience and admiration which cannot be claimed by any monarch in Europe. This is partly based on the awareness of his people that they owe him everything. Through revelations, as he says, he showed them the right spot for their settlement, planned the city, built houses for them, constructed water pipelines and created any other necessities for their community life (many insufficient of course).

Driving into the city you will find a sign above each store: Holiness to the Lord, Zions Co-operative Mercantile Institution. That was also started by Brigham Young. "The Church" sold shares for $25 each and built stores whose gains profit the Church and the stockholders in equal parts. Store managers are Church employees and have a fixed salary paid by the general funds. Any stores that do not have this inscription (the sun of the Trinity is generally added to it) are owned by gentiles and are ignored. Most of the co-operative stores are supposedly doing splendid business, especially since immigrants, adventurers, and mine explorers passing through buy what they need for their travels here.

The education of the children is a high priority; there are numerous elementary schools in which the tuition is free. They have plans for a so-called university, where certain lectures have already been started, in living and dead languages, higher mathematics, etc. Small post offices, telegraph offices, parcel shipping, and supply stores have been established in which the students can be prepared for their future professions. For all these miniature commercial institutions, the university prints its own paper money, stamps, and tax stamps that are distributed to the students and are used to regulate transactions. I will bring along some of this paper money and stamps. I will also bring some Mormon religious books that will no doubt interest you.

Nature has made it possible for the inhabitants of Salt Lake City to make everything they need themselves or at least produce it in the area of Utah. They make their own theater costumes, the decorations, the organ in the Tabernacle (which supposedly consists of 300 pipes), the paper for their newspapers. The marble for the embellishment of the houses and the coal for heating are brought from close by. It almost seems that they have no need of the rest of the world. There is neither real poverty nor great riches. The average inhabitant can be called well-to-do. Some guess that Brigham Young as their Croesus owns a fortune of $500,000, some say only half as much. Nobody knows for sure.

I won't be able to provide more details today because it is time for the Sunday service at the Tabernacle. Just a few words about Brigham Young. We found him in his "office," where Hooper introduced us with an air of deep submissiveness. He is close to 70 years old, but looks as though he were in the mid-50s, is substantial, a little above medium height, with grayish blond hair. His gray eyes look rather strict and cunning without being unpleasant. Our friends said later that the president may have been tired; I just found him quiet and calm, his speech almost inaudible. His face moved only once, when I mentioned how the people on the train had treated the goods meant for Salt Lake City with little concern. This seemed to make him angry. I asked whether he found the train unpleasant because it brought so many foreign elements into his area. He denied that and told us that he was planning a second train line from Ogden to here and had started this project already. I do believe that he puts a good face on a not-so-good business and is smart enough to take the initiative in this matter, which would have been enforced by the train company or the government sooner or later. It can't be in his interest to "corrupt" his people by contact with strangers, and I am convinced that any stranger, including us, is a thorn in his side. (Indeed we bring certain bad habits with us as this example shows: The Mormons drink hardly anything except water even though they are not forbidden to drink anything else. When we asked for wine in our hotel last night there was none. They offered to get some of this contemptible beverage from the gentile store; we refused with pride, but went to buy a couple of bottles in such a store and had a glass secretly in our room in the evening with the Frenchman. Not to offend, we quickly hid the remains and glasses under our bed when we heard the maid approach unexpectedly.)

Yesterday we took a carriage trip to the Salt Lake. The old overland mail road leads through the desert as soon as it leaves the city. Every 20 or 30 steps we saw the head or skeleton of a weather-bleached ox or horse carcass in the sand or dry grass; since there are so many, nobody takes the time to bury them. If they fall over dead on the journey, they get lugged to the side of the road and left there. With such clear markers, it's hard to miss the road! When we reached the lake after about four hours, we saw the tropical colors again, on the snowy mountains, near and far away, and on the many rocky islands in the lake. The landscape offered a most beautiful and grandiose sight from the place on the southern shore where we were standing. If this view is exceeded by anything, it would be by the sunsets we have witnessed from the city in the last two days.

The water of the lake is much saltier than the ocean and people say that swimming in it is difficult because you get pushed to the surface. Where and whether this lake has an outlet has not been discovered. The tributaries are all sweet water, and the biggest one is the Jordan River, which passes through the city. Close to the lake is the lone house of a Mormon, where we were fed excellently well. It was especially pleasant after the long and difficult drive through the dead desert even if "violets a la Huster" were not on the menu. The inhabitants of the settlement have a harmonium and New York magazines and converse pleasantly in an educated way. All of this in the wilderness! Brigham Young does have an extraordinary genius for civilizing his subjects. I have to quote one expression of our Mormon about this interesting man. When I casually mentioned that we had met both presidents of America, who have such famous names, he said in reference to Grant's former activities in the war: "The one is great at killing men, and the other is great at producing children." The number of Young's children is not known!

Tomorrow morning at 4:00 we go on to San Francisco, where we plan to arrive Wednesday evening, July 21. It is too bad that I can't write you about the Tabernacle today. For your amusement I will tell you another peculiarity of the Mormons: when they hold public formal dances they use the churches, moving the chairs to the side. The musicians stand on the preacher's podium. What would St. Stephen[63] say to that?

Occidental Hotel[64]
San Francisco, July 22, 1869

It looks as though we had arrived at our final destination healthy and happy. I have to say again and again: What a trip! How interesting! How new! Imagine—we are as far as the Occident usually extends in our world and the next country across the Pacific is already our East!

California is a different world from the "States," and the two high mountain ranges, the Rocky Mountains and the Sierra Nevada, which separate California from the rest of the United States, are not only a geographic division but part of the character and the way of life of its inhabitants. For today, I will not undertake to describe this strange and remarkable fact nor the impression San Francisco made on me; I will write a separate essay in honor of this important subject. This essay will follow in a few days. For the time being I will wrap up our final day with the Mormons and the last stretch of the Pacific Railway trip.

Soon after I finished the previous letter (as you know it was on a Sunday), we went to the service in what is called the Tabernacle, a big building of singular construction which from the outside resembles more a heathen temple than a Christian church. Inside it looks like a reformed church—barren, no pictures or other ornaments. The only half-finished Tabernacle was filled with about 4,000 people. The president, the patriarch, two vice presidents, the bishops, and elders and apostles of the "Latter-day-Saints" were seated on a raised area of the Tabernacle at one end, beneath the organ. Each speaker gets up from their midst. In front of them, six people prepare communion on a long table while people sing hymns at the start of the service. Neither the people nor the speaker nor the President wear churchlike clothes. They don their usual suits, some not even with dark coats.

The communion, taken every Sunday, consists of bread and water: Wine will only be introduced when it is possible to produce it in Salt Lake City itself. They are working on this project eagerly and everywhere. It is one of the "revelations" of God to Brigham Young that Mormons should not drink foreign wine for their communion. Twelve big silver-plated baskets are filled with bread and are given to the community with as many porcelain pitchers of water. Each member takes a sip of water and a bite of bread and hands the pitcher and basket to his neighbor. Thus they get passed around before being put on the table again. All this happens at the beginning of the sermon.

In my opinion, it is a strange and remarkable custom that the Mormon elders will give a chance to preach to any preacher of any Christian sect who is traveling through the city and asks for this favor. This proves that they are quite sure of their people. Brigham tends to add comments of his own, after someone from other parts has spoken, in which he comments on this sermon and tells his community what they should approve of and what not. This does not necessarily happen in a complimentary way if the speaker has voiced heretical views. This time we heard the sermon of a Methodist preacher. We enjoyed the fact that Brigham Young's usual comments after the sermon were rather polite to the Methodist. Brigham speaks without artifice and not like an educated man, but with a special emphasis which has an extraordinary effect, especially on women. He combines assertions and principles without giving a reason or defending them, just presents them as laws accepted by the community with humility as coming from the mouth of a saint. The topics of his speech were the main principles of the Mormon religion, not including polygamy. The sermon of the Methodist preacher took one hour, Young's a half hour. The service ended, as it had started, with two or three hymns.

In the evening, we visited our Mormon for a little while and were received in a friendly manner by him and his wife. As I told you earlier, I regret that he does not have a dozen wives for our amusement. We conversed about their religion and, not for the first time, I was astonished how deeply their beliefs were rooted in the hearts of Brigham's disciples. They talk about it all with calm conviction and certainty, and I am convinced that they would again leave their self-made settlement, should it be necessary, in order to cultivate another desert. There are the occasional rumors that the colony of Latter-Day Saints might be moved further west to the Sandwich Islands, probably in response to the changes wrought by the Pacific Railway. This was the end of our memorable stay at the salt water lake; at 3:30 the next morning we entered the Wells Fargo and Co. coach again and arrived in Uintah at 10:00 a.m.

I am starting to think that even America is small. On our trip from Uintah to Salt Lake City, I met an English lord who had crossed with us on the *Scotia*; in the coach from Salt Lake City to Uintah I was surprised by the company of two young ladies whom I had seen in Washington and who remembered me also as I could tell from their gestures after we had met each other formally. They are from St. Louis and belong to a large group of travelers who include among others the mayor of St. Louis by the name of Cole, the Methodist preacher O. H. Tiffany, memorable from the Tabernacle, and Senator Harlan (formerly Secretary of the Interior). We traveled in the same car with all of them and entertained ourselves very pleasantly. The entire group is also staying in the Occidental Hotel.

At 11:00 in the morning, we boarded the Union Pacific Railway and arrived at its end point in Promontory at 3:00 p.m. This is where the Central Pacific Railroad of California starts (the full title of this train) and we were lucky enough to book a stateroom in the sleeping car. I had ordered it in advance by telegram because I suspected problems due to the number of travelers—and I was right. The large group had also reserved in advance. We were the only ones besides this group who managed to find room in the sleeping car. The rest of the passengers had to take the regular compartments till Sacramento, not an enviable position. Our trip was almost merrier yet than on the Union Pacific Railway; we traded a lot of nonsense with the ladies, talked and played, and had picnics with our respective food baskets. In the evening the young girls sang for us under the direction of the mayor, who turned out to be a great musician and gave the beat with a fork while we stood on the platform breathing the delightfully cool air and watching the full moon which, as in Italy, shone with a special brightness. Occasionally when we had to stop to supply the engine with water, Chinese workers congregated around our car wondering about the melodic sounds emanating from it, and I took pleasure in lighting up some of these Mongolian faces with gratitude by handing them a glass of red wine.

Our general cheerfulness was partly based on the relatively good condition of the tracks. Even though the Central Pacific train cannot be compared to our trains we felt more secure on it than on the Union Pacific trains. It looks as if on this side of the Rocky Mountains the work was more careful in order to produce something a little more durable. The railroad ties here are carved while the ones on the Union Pacific track were simple tree trunks which were cut down and put on the tracks at certain distances, which naturally made the tracks rather uneven. The embankments and the rocky clefts are wider, and while the bridges are still made of wood, they are of better construction. In addition, the difficult terrain of the Union Pacific Railway cannot be compared with that of the Central Pacific Railway. Even though the pass over the Rocky Mountains was higher than across the Sierra Nevada Mountains, you will have noticed from my descriptions that the ascent to the Rocky Mountains was rather gradual and only required extraordinary engineering feats in one stretch. In contrast, the train across the Sierra Nevada is a masterwork of engineering science and art from beginning to end. We saw great viaducts and embankments constantly; sometimes we passed high rocks, sometimes deep crevices and abysses, traveling alternately uphill and downhill. I must compliment the driver of the locomotive for proceeding so carefully and not going faster than a common carriage across the entire Sierra Nevada. In places like the Cap Horn, where we were looking down from the window into a valley 2,000 feet below, the travelers were especially grateful.

The fact that this train track was built so much more carefully is not in small part due to the Chinese workers. They are more diligent than the other workers (who as you know are "gentlemen") and in addition demand less pay. They are still to be found at many parts of the track, repairing what is necessary. Sometimes we see hundreds of these droll fellows greeting the train with joyous screams and swinging hats when we pass their camps; it is obvious that they enjoy their work and are proud of it.

Things look like a fantasy on this Pacific train! Whites, Negroes, Chinese, Indians, Mormons, people of all languages and nations, gold, silver, copper, and mercury miners, adventurers of all kinds. Everyone takes this transport back and forth; the adventurers increase in number the closer we get to California. They have discovered several new mines recently; a main attraction at the moment is the one in White Pine, Arizona, which has been mined for only a few months and is supposed to hold large quantities of silver; several others rich in precious metals were found in Idaho. This is why we see signs at many stations saying "To the new mines." In such places, there are usually six- or eight-span coaches that transport the miners—mostly young, bold fellows, tall as trees and of strong constitution—hundreds of miles into the wilderness to their destination. Here everyone wears pistols and guns since new mines also attract new villains and people need weapons to defend themselves against those as well as against the Indians who live in great numbers north and south of the train line. We caught sight of some of them in several places.

The area is dreary until the base of the Sierra. For two days and nights we passed through uninterrupted desert, on average 4,000 feet above sea level, the barometer showing 23.9″. We passed only one sparse waterway on this endless stretch, the Humboldt River, which eventually disappears in the sand. On both banks of this river you can find a bit of grass and low bushes; that's how we could follow it into the distance with our eyes— nothing green can be seen anywhere else. We watched it with longing. Everywhere else there is nothing but bare ground, covered with whitish alkali that makes a fine penetrating dust which is very, very unpleasant and can't be avoided, since it never rains here. Our noses felt sore, eyes and mouth became completely dry, and lack of fresh drinking water was all the more noticeable because the water we brought along spoiled in the hot sun and could only be made drinkable by adding sufficient amounts of brandy or whiskey.

On the second day, the monotonous desert was occasionally disrupted by imposing mountains, the Humboldt Range. Upon waking on the third day, we were surprised by the appearance of the high Sierra Nevada cov- ered with fir trees. The area takes on a completely different character. The vegetation becomes more and more lush. At the stops, people are selling wonderful fruit, peaches of a size I had never seen before. We traveled through gorges with wild and romantic panoramas alternating—a most beautiful stretch. Special barriers have been erected against avalanches and the train had to pass through wooden tunnels for 23 miles, the so- called snow sheds, which unfortunately were not advantageous for the viewer. At the end, we could see the famous gold mines of Flat Valley far below us in the valley along whose rim we passed. We also saw the aque- ducts disposing of the yellow water that had been used to wash the gold. This is where we noticed that we had arrived in the land of gold!

At 1:00 p.m., punctually according to schedule, we reached Sacramento, the endpoint of the Pacific Railway, after an expedition of more than two days and two nights from Salt Lake City. We immediately boarded an elegant steamship like the ones on the Hudson and traveled down the Sacramento River for eight hours, then passed the Bays of Suisun, Pablo, and San Francisco, finally landing here around 10 o'clock in the evening.

As soon as we boarded the ship and entered our private rooms we changed our clothes, which had taken on a rather indeterminate color, due to the desert dust, and I joyfully put myself into the hands of the ship's barber (a German, of course), who managed to make my face human again. The change from train to steamship had already been very pleasant, and the parching heat that had reigned during the day on our trip and increased to a truly unendurable degree in Sacramento diminished more and more on the water as we approached the Pacific Ocean. I will tell you about the wonderful temperature in San Francisco with the next letter.

We are excellently taken care of here. The Occidental Hotel is one of the best in the United States, and Mr. Hawkins, brother of the young widow whom we met on the Union Pacific Railway, had ordered our quarters and had recommended us to the landlord. When we left the ship, I found a man who asked if I was Mr. Mendelssohn and when I assented he took us to a waiting coach. It was pleasant to find someone in such a distant place who knew how to address me by name.

Occidental Hotel
San Francisco, July 27, 1869

The enclosed men, photographed as typical Californians, send you their pictures with best wishes. As you can see, the costume of the two is appropriate for the heat, the posture typical for a Yankee, and it is terrible but true that they wear their hats this way in real life.

Since my last letter to you, I have received three of yours and am in heaven, having long missed our communications. You laud me for the details of my reports, and Father comments on the ease with which I write them. This is undeserved, especially praise for my ease in writing. My letters are not nearly as detailed as the ones from Scotland. I want to convince you that, contrary to your impression, they are written in haste and superficially, since otherwise the bad form, the deletions, and the almost unreadable handwriting could not be excused. Worse than the surface of my letters, the haste is affecting their contents. I am afraid I often give in to subjective pronouncements. I start developing a viewpoint with a remark, get carried away into a wide range of subjects, then somehow wrap it up because time is running out. I often judge things too fast, quite natural for the lively pace of this trip. I am well aware of these conditions and mean to show you the reasons.

You know that it is my joy and endeavor to report my first views of the scenery and landscapes as quickly as possible. The same is true for my impressions of any new situations and conditions. I therefore don't have time to study and follow them up, but report them to you at first glance, so to speak. Whether they were right or wrong is as unpredictable and coincidental as always in life. Sometimes I perceive something as an error shortly after I have written it down. But to correct what is already written is too complicated and I therefore avoid it. Frequently I find it enjoyable to see that I come to the right point of view gradually as I orient myself to the character of people and things. Naturally I feel justified if what I had judged as strange and American, as advantageous or disadvantageous, is confirmed by people who have lived here for a long time and are very familiar with everything. I also maintain that Tocqueville's book[65] is likely more interesting if read after the trip than before. I will then be able to compare it with my own impressions, which were conceived without outside help, even if they contain mistakes. This way at least I don't have a guide who is not likely to let me approach things without prejudice.

The day after our arrival we spent with the oft-mentioned widow whom we also met on the next day at a pitiful concert from which we accompanied her home. We spent another hour together drinking native champagne, toasting each other's health. Today we will visit her again, not having been there for four long (!) days. I am giving one of her sisters a collection of German songs to educate her taste. Hardly anything other than Verdi is known in these parts, and it is a significant comment on the musical education that the beauty does not even know what kind of animal a string quartet is!

I would ponder this more if my time were not taken up admiring San Francisco, likely the strangest spot in the world and completely different from everything else we have seen so far. I need to talk about what interests me most in this most cosmopolitan of all cities: the Chinese and their life. The Chinese live in a quarter all by themselves. There one meets almost exclusively people of their tribe, the stores in the area all run in Chinese. Walking through the business district in the evening, we see them working behind their counters, adding up what they have earned and painting their special characters into very clean and dainty-looking books with their hair hanging all the way down to the floor in long braids. They write with brushes, usually with the left hand, held between the third and fourth fingers, and with their special ink.

It's well known that the Chinese are excellent businessmen and sometimes first-rate rogues (see *Merkur* 70). A few of them become rich but are not likely to stay here once they do; they prefer to return to their native land. Here they are all hated, despised, and treated as enemies. The reasons are simple: As workers they do their job for little money, something the others, especially the Irish, would rather do for considerably more. Naturally the competitive bitterness of the so-called working classes of the other races is considerable, and it is feared that this will become a very difficult and burning issue shortly, especially since the number of Chinese increases steadily. While voices from the East have suggested introducing descendants of Confucius as servants there also, the fury of the others has increased dramatically. Impartial people admit that there are no better and more conscientious workers than the Chinese. They are excellent servants; they have a monopoly on laundry in California and also work as cooks. Those wanting to get rid of them argue that they spoil the area with their vices—a theme which, for various reasons, I would rather tell you about in person.

It makes a curious impression to see the neighborhoods I am telling you about with all signs, leaflets, and announcements in the Chinese language and characters. The names of the company written above the stores are usually also spelled out in English as well. I am writing some of these down because of their peculiarity: Yan On Shong & Co; Yee Wo; Wing Fung & Co.; Wong Wing; Wing Wau; and on and on with the Wings, Waus, Wongs, Shongs into infinity. The Chinese also run two theaters and two temples. I will write about the first later; the latter I have not seen yet. Everything is highly amusing and original: their customary dress, the shoes curved upward, the handsomely braided long hair that they wrap around their otherwise shaved heads while they are doing hard work. I have witnessed repeatedly how they shave their heads with strangely formed half-moon-like knives, a service they lovingly provide for each other.

Although the men look pleasant with their braids and white shirts (which they tend to wear at home, especially those specializing in laundry), the women look disgusting; they are made up beyond words, walking awkwardly on crippled feet in a kind of shoe that should make them fall on their noses at any moment. Some wear braids like the men, some national fan-shaped hair styles, colossal in contrast to their small stature. The wives of the rich merchants never show themselves in the street and rarely leave the house, a custom the few proper women also share.

It is more difficult for me to distinguish between the Chinese than it was between Negroes, a problem I have mentioned earlier. The Chinese really all look like the same man, or more likely the same woman, because their faces are not very manly. It is my chief pleasure to watch their lives and activities here. I visit their quarter at least twice a day and spend time observing them.

But there is plenty to see in the city: the extensive bay with the many big ships leaving for all parts of the world, the liveliness of the streets, the peculiar position of the city on sandy hills which make us wander up and down hills like in Rome. The many fruits offered at the corners make a pretty picture. They are miraculous in size and taste. Fruits of all seasons: apples, strawberries, peaches, nuts, apricots, grapes, plums, and pears, in short all you can think of are available all year round without interruption. The quality and variety of the vegetables is the same; I have seen potatoes of the size of a child's head. There cannot be anything prettier for a housewife than the look of the market halls with all the fruits and vegetables, with big fish from the Pacific, many of which are not known to me by name or appearance. Oysters are also available all year long. As everywhere in the American coastal cities, they are consumed in different ways: fried, scrambled, stewed, pickled, scalloped, and so on to infinity. It seems amusing to me that I am now able to say that the oysters of the Atlantic are superior to those of the Pacific!

In a sense, a common language does not exist in San Francisco; one hears languages of all nations, after English especially Spanish, also German and Italian, but less French. The climate is very strange and completely different from the rest of California. San Francisco is special in that it is situated on a peninsula which receives the breeze of the ocean from the west and that of the bay from the east. The Golden Gate, the small opening which connects the bay with the ocean, north of the city, cuts through the mountainous coastline and causes a consistent strong current of wind that serves to spread coolness. July and August tend to be the relatively coolest months here; they have the most unpleasant winds, bring fog, and are the real winter for San Francisco. The sun is very pleasant and not too warm—a great contrast to the temperatures which we have had to bear with so far. In the morning and evening, we would catch cold without a coat. During what we call winter, it is supposed to be even more pleasant because the warmth is greater even though the temperature stays the same. Mr. Hawkins told me that he could wear the same suit all year long.

It never rains between the beginning of April and the end of October. Umbrellas can be stowed during that time. Dust is an unpleasant problem caused by the strong winds on the sandy soil and untamed by any moisture, reminding us of our chief suffering on the Pacific train. We really noticed the difference between here and the interior yesterday and the day before when we undertook an excursion to the great mercury mines of New Almaden in the County of Santa Clara. We took the train to San Jose (50 miles from here) and a carriage for about 15 miles toward the south, to the mines on top of a mountain. There we descended into a deep shaft, led by Spanish guides; I took some of the mercury ore, mined in front of our eyes, along for you. The following curious thing happened there: When we had descended all the way to a small hole at the furthest point the miners had explored, the men working there made a deafening noise with their tools and stood in a circle around us to prevent us from leaving. We understood the meaning of this joke and bought our freedom from the underworld with some dollars, as the noise in this small space was hard to endure.

The mercury ore is distilled in big chambers, dried rather than melted; the resulting vapor is conducted through a series of empty chambers, getting cooler and cooler, until it condenses and the pure mercury is obtained. It continually drips down the walls of the chamber, is caught in big vats and immediately filled into metal bottles, each containing 76½ pounds, and sent off. The mercury ore consists of serpentine, cinnabar, and sulfur; nowadays it contains 12 to 13% mercury, formerly it is supposed to have contained more than 60%.

Close to the mines there is a spring that produces a great amount of excellent soda water. The overseer of the mines, to our joy a Berliner by the name of F., took us there when we expressed the wish to enjoy a glass of water. Nature has provided abundantly for this country. The Almaden Vichy Water (the name of this spring) is only used to refresh the few miners. Hardly anyone knows of its existence elsewhere!

For today I must close. One more word of admiration for the Pacific Ocean: the beach can be reached in a half-hour trip across the peninsula to the west. We caught the first glimpse of it from the top of a cliff where the path ends at the Cliff House, a famous entertainment place for the inhabitants of San Francisco. Close to the shore are three little islands made of bare rock; two of them are completely covered with pelicans and sea birds and the third is inhabited by seals, playing with each other and barking loudly. Beyond them there is nothing but the endless sea. We climbed down to the beach and were astonished that we could find hardly any shells, as far as the eye could see. It is as if the Pacific were too serious for this kind of playfulness of nature. We could only collect a few, all of one kind, of different sizes, all strong and solid.

Occidental Hotel
San Francisco, July 29, 1869

In a few hours we are planning to make a big excursion into the interior, mainly to Yosemite Valley (as the Americans say: the most beautiful place on earth. As you have noticed, they tend to equate "earth" with "United States"), to colossal waterfalls, huge trees (the Big Trees), in short to all kinds of miracles. The tour will take 10 to 12 days during which you should not expect any letters from me. We will return here directly from the Yosemite Valley. Then you will receive a giant letter, in proper relation to the wonders awaiting us in this valley. I expect the expedition to be very interesting. I will have many things to report. We leave on a 13-hour boat trip up the San Joaquin River to Stockton. From there, partly by carriage, partly by horse, we will proceed to the interior of the Sierra where the valley is. We are renting the four-legged and two-legged workers for the entire time. We will sleep, eat, and stay where everyone sleeps, eats, and stays. More later after the work is done!

Yesterday we attended one of the two Chinese theaters, the larger one in Jackson Street. It was the funniest evening I ever experienced! The entire place was crammed exclusively with Chinese who attend the performance, which I have heard lasts from 7:00 in the evening till 3:00 in the morning, tirelessly from beginning to end; we were the only representatives of the Caucasian race. The musicians consisted of a gong beater (the gong is a metal plate which is hit with a cotton-padded mallet), another musician who kept hitting a kind of wooden anvil with two wooden mallets (a deafening noise), and several other virtuosos on instruments I had never seen or heard of—all competing to see who could make the biggest spectacle—standing on the stage right behind the actors. During the "songs" the gong player puts away his instruments and, to accompany the singers, takes up another instrument whose sound is a strange cross between violin and bagpipe. The piece was a historical tragedy (as explained to me by an adept in the Chinese language sitting next to me; for me it could have been just a ballet with voice). Long arias, conversations, and monologues occurred with great frequency. As soon as someone said "Tsching, Tschu, na ko sang sing" or something similar, the musical spectacle started again, then again Tsching, Tschang, then music, and so on until our ears hurt. The actors yelled their words with shrill voices and, when they became emotional, they jumped and wiggled around madly, almost as in an epileptic fit. The costumes were magnificent, made of heavy silk in the most beautiful colors. In the loges we noticed some of the Chinese swells who looked as blasé as our European ones, while the plebeians in the stalls showed their interest in the performance with lively gestures and cries. Too bad that I can't give you more detail today. It is late at night and I must have a few hours of sleep. After our return we will attend another couple of Chinese Theater productions. Then I will continue the description.

Occidental Hotel
San Francisco, August 10, 1869
Dear family, I greet you joyfully, back in San Francisco again. To be honest, both Ernst and I are rather glad that the almost 14-day tour is happily over. It was a strain from beginning to end. But we are both healthy, quite sunburned, and richer by many strange sights and experiences—*gaudeamus!* In parentheses, I must explain that the concept and plan of our expedition was thanks to Mr. G. who lives here and whose acquaintance we had made in the German Club. Now forward!

Equipped solely with a duster and the so-called saddlebags (two connected bags stowed behind the saddle while riding)—no rain as I told you the other day, so no umbrellas necessary—we boarded the steamship on Thursday, July 29, back along the route we had taken earlier through the bays of San Francisco, Pablo, and Suisun, the confluence of the Sacramento and the San Joaquin rivers and up the San Joaquin during the following night, to Stockton. We slept till morning in our berth on the ship and debarked at 6:00 a.m. Spending much time trying to find a conveyance, of which there were plenty, but with no driver willing to take us, we finally managed to get a two-horse carriage with a driver who undertook to transport us the 160 miles to Mariposa for 75 gold dollars. From there we will start riding on horseback.

We now left Stockton and immediately enjoyed the blazing sun of California, which has a right to its name and from which only San Francisco is shielded. On cool days it was 28° in the shade while we were in the interior. In the sun, the thermometer showed 38 to 42°, and that is where we were almost exclusively.

There is nothing more awful than the trip from Stockton to Mariposa, which takes 36 hours, excluding the overnight stops. Not a tree on the entire road. The sun burns almost like the flame of a hydrogen torch. Since it has not rained for several months, dust covers the ground a foot thick and envelops the happy traveler from beginning to end in a cloud that no air current will blow away. We could hardly breathe and found ourselves covered with a thick crust within a few hours. As regards cleanliness, it must be completely given up for the duration of this excursion.

On the entire stretch to Mariposa we saw sand and nothing but sand, no elevation of the ground, a farm every 20 miles or so. The only diversions were the stops at the ferries across several streams, of which the Stanislaus, Tuolumne, and Merced rivers are the important ones. Of course, bridges do not exist in this highly cultivated corner of the world. We had to entrust ourselves and our vehicle to more or less fragile conveyances, usually of strange construction, altogether neglecting the rules of the art of shipbuilding. These barks were usually burdened with large carts bringing the products of civilization to the settlers strewn around the country. They often travel in long trains and are usually drawn by 12 or 16 donkeys who are transported by ship with great difficulty and commotion.

Frequently we had the pleasure of waiting for half an hour in the sun and were happy if it did not take longer. The few "inns" on the way were pitiful, unappetizing huts. The saloon was usually shared with feathery creatures who competed in soiling the floor with the tobacco-spitting workers (my friends, the gentlemen) taking their siesta at any time of day. So we often had a hard time finding a place to step, never mind to sit down. Of course, the driver, like all the other gentlemen and later our guide, would sit at the same table with us. No traveler in this country should expect anything different. He needs to be happy to be served at all. The latter business is the task of the Chinese.

The inn we stayed at in Snellings, at the end of the first day, after a trip of 65 miles, was a little better than the ones on the way. Coulter, the landlord, who told us that he had settled here a few years ago to rest from his achievement of founding the "big city" of Coulterville a few days' trip from here, took pains with us, and on his recommendation we changed our plans for the next day. Instead of proceeding the 41 miles to Mariposa directly, we took a detour to the gold mines of Bear Valley and thus saw something we should not have missed before leaving California.

On arriving in Bear Valley we contacted the supervisor of the mines, a certain Mr. Rice, who showed us all around and explained the extraction of gold, from breaking off the quartz to finally annealing the gold particles. Every day they process about 35 tons of quartz (about 35,000 kg); each ton delivers an average yield of $20 to $30, an arduous business! Everything is handled exclusively by Chinese workers. There is a kind of quartz mill which is revolutionary for gold diggers. In a pleasant coincidence its inventor, a certain Mr. Ryerson, happened to be present at Bear Valley and took us by horseback to the Benton Mills four miles away, where we were able to see it in action. The process of obtaining gold which we witnessed there is as follows: The quartz pieces are crushed into a whitish powder by a water-powered mill. This powder is mixed in great vats with mercury, which amalgamates with the gold particles. Then the contents of the vats are exposed to a thin jet of water in a curious washing apparatus which washes away the light stones and leaves the heavier amalgamate. The latter is then put in retorts and heated, which makes the mercury evaporate and leaves the pure gold.

On the way back from the mills we passed a Chinese village where the workers live, then an Indian camp. We thought it strange, on arriving

back in Bear Valley, to see a pretty white face again when Mr. Rice introduced us to his dainty young wife. She had heard that a "nephew of Uncle"
was present and wanted to make our acquaintance. Even there! Some of
her friends and their husbands, with whom we conversed pleasantly, also
joined us. When it was getting dark and we climbed into our vehicle to
drive the 12 miles to Mariposa, the farewells were endless.

On the whole, as you can see, those first two days of our trip were already rather strenuous. The first day, we were on the road from 8:00 in the
morning to 9:00 in the evening; on the second, we were in the carriage
from 6:00 to 2:00, and again from 7:00 to 9:00; in between, we rode eight
miles on horseback and walked around the mills. The fact that our driver
had no idea of the directions (no real roads anyway) and that three times
we had to ask for directions from farmers we luckily ran into and then
change our course, is pretty natural under the conditions here. It is not so
natural that our cart did not once fall over and that we arrived at the places
we had meant to in the evenings. But our poor horses! To have to walk
65 miles on the first day and 41 on the second seems like cruelty to animals,
but the rest of the trip made us less sensitive to such selfless thoughts.

Third Day

In Mariposa, a terribly hot little nest consisting of a few wooden houses
(can be found on a detailed map, southeast of Stockton), we were glad
to separate from our plagued creatures and their driver (who by the way
could not be stopped from inviting us for a drink, after receiving our
tip with dignity, and telling us how much the acquaintance with us had
pleased him). He immediately hired the necessary horses and a guide
for our expedition to the Big Trees and the Yosemite Valley. We have to
pay a daily fee for this guide and also for his horses and their keep. The
horses are a Mexican/Californian mixed breed, small and ugly, but, as
we were told, of great strength and endurance; the guide, Mister Peter
Gordon (etiquette demands we call him that; using the English custom
of Sir contradicts the republican principles and may never be used), was
recommended to us by G. and turned out to be beyond reproach. Thus we
were well taken care of in all respects.

At 7:30 in the morning we got started; we aimed at covering 24 miles
on that day. In the middle of the stretch we planned to have two hours

of quiet at a small friendly ranch (a term one uses here often instead of *farm*), but otherwise, no stops. At first, we took a path which had a distant similarity to a road; after about 14 miles, we left this road and traveled on a trail that it was hard not to leave since it often became invisible. It was exceedingly strenuous, visible or invisible. It led up and down hills which seemed impossible to climb since they were so steep; across stony stretches where we feared for our horses; through creeks in which we frequently got wetter than intended, even though the closeness of water was pleasant in the blazing heat. The horses would like standing in the creeks for a few seconds, taking quick draughts of water, and the riders followed their good example. For our refreshment we had flasks around our necks filled with brandy, a small sip of which often gave us strength; a few drops mixed with water also helped to disable any bad effects. The customary Mexican saddles, the only kind used in the West and often used elsewhere in the States, are a great convenience; their leather-covered stirrups are especially good protection for feet and legs to keep them dry when riding through the creeks.

We only caught sight of our stop for the night in the evening. It was a little wooden hut named for its owner, as is the custom in all these lonely areas; it is called Clark's.[66] We stayed at this elevation of about 4,129 feet for two nights, since we were to visit the Big Trees from here before traveling on into the valley. I regret to report that these two nights, even though they were not disturbed by the rattling of wheels, did not bring us the refreshing rest we had hoped for. They were disturbed by Father's special friends, the bedbugs, which attacked us in hordes and hunted around us like the mice around Bishop Hatto[67] in the olden days.

But the day between the two lost nights compensated us for great sufferings and would have made up for even greater ones. If the seven wonders of the world really exist, the Big Trees should certainly be number eight. Imagine a group of 660 trees, each several hundred feet high, the thickest of them 104 feet in diameter at the base! The lowest branches of this last giant, which start about 90 feet above the ground, have a diameter of 6½ feet. One of the trunks fell over and was burned out by Indians: it is roomy enough for a house. The most striking feature is that these trees all grow straight as a candle, the branches in harmonious relation to the trunk and gradually becoming less thick, all the way to the top of the tree. The crowns are partly broken, likely by the weight of the snow they bear each year, which means several thousand times already (their age according to the rings). The trunks are almost all damaged by Indian fires at the base. This is a singular species of tree called *Wellingtonia gigantea* in the plant kingdom. They exist nowhere else except in California, and here only in two places, Mariposa and Calaveras Counties.

All the trees in this part of the Sierra grow wonderfully straight from bottom to top, like the Big Trees. They are often just as high, only not as wide. One of the trees in front of our Yosemite Valley hut is 209 feet high. These are usually common or sugar pines, which bear extraordinarily long pine cones; the biggest one I saw was only a little shorter than two feet. It is therefore not recommended to travel in this area in the season when they fall down! In addition, there are many other more or less rare trees here, such as mahogany or manzanita trees. They all grow 6,000 to 7,000 feet above sea level. Even above 8,000 feet we traveled through a thick fir woods! The giant trees are at a level of about 6,000 feet; the distance from Clark's is six miles. That day we covered about 15 miles. The next day was the most strenuous of the entire tour. We had to ride 24 miles to get to the final destination of our expedition, to reach the Yosemite (Indian for "gray bear") Valley. Twenty-four miles are quite a nice piece of work for horse and rider on level ground, but under the conditions I have described already, they seemed an eternity. Many times we had to travel several thousand feet up and down again; we often had to get off to pull our reluctant horses up or down the steep slopes, which was neither easy nor pleasant in the blazing heat and the endless dust we sank into past our ankles. We can't even say that we rode slowly; as the terrain permitted, we galloped or trotted across sticks and stones. One curiosity I must still mention: we came across a place called Westphal's Meadow. Someone called Westphal supposedly retreated into this lonely area with his Chinese wife and lived here for a few years. American customs frown on such mixed-race marriages, and anyone sinning against this code is banned from society.

In nine and one half hours (including a short rest for lunch in the shade of a magnificent tree), we reached the valley. Knowing how enthusiastic Californians are about the natural beauty of this valley, one would generally find it exaggerated. Californians and others—who might avoid showing a different opinion out of politeness—call it the most beautiful place in the world. Even Schlaginweit, who has traveled around the world and seen the Himalayas, the Caucasus, and the Alps, confirmed this judgment at the German Club in San Francisco, saying that he had not seen such beautiful nature in any part of the world.

I have to admit that I find this valley *more grandiose* than anything else I know and that, to show a comparison with scenery familiar to you, the valleys of Switzerland are not up to par with the Yosemite Valley; however, those Swiss valleys are rarely without some loveliness and grace, a character completely missing here. Of course, the Yosemite Valley has the grandiosity of an interesting original wilderness; you can see that most of the places in this valley have not been touched by human feet. This is because it was only recently discovered when settlers of the plains were attacked and murdered by Indian tribes. Their friends gathered in great numbers to avenge them and followed the retreating Indians all the way into this valley, from which the Indians could not escape fast enough and where a terrible battle took place, destroying all the redskins. From this time the area has become known and has been visited more and more. Measures of the height, length, and width of this valley are still imprecise. The following is supposed to be an approximation: the valley itself is 4,100 feet above sea level, the length is nine and one half miles, its greatest width, three quarters of a mile. It is surrounded by mountains 7,000 to 10,000 feet high, with walls of completely bare rock rising vertically so that access is only possible in a few places. Seeing these walls rise 3,000 to 6,000 feet straight as a candle is a rare and grandiose view. Two waterfalls of extraordinary dimensions flow down from them, in addition to several smaller ones. One of them is called Pohono in Indian and Bridal Falls in English; it falls without interruption for 900 feet. The other, Yosemite Falls, drops 2,700 feet in two sections, one 1,600 feet, the other 1,100. Just opposite this falls, in front of the giant tree before the hut, at the foot of one of the largest boulders, is our "hotel," a loosely boarded, long hut which became our quarters for two days.

In front of this palace you can see two Europeans, sitting in woolen shirts without collar or vest, just covered in linen dusters, hats (huge native Panama hats) pushed as far back as possible, covered in nameless dirt. They are conversing with the two male inhabitants of the house, a strong Yankee and a Swede who deserted as an eleven-year-old ship's boy and is now traipsing around California as a "gentleman." Such figures outfitted in high boots, woolen shirts, and trousers, with no other accessories, are common in all of California. In their belts they carry a big knife and revolver, which gets aimed every few moments at a passing bird or Indian dog that disturbs the grazing cattle of the farm, or even at a trout in the passing creek (barbarism to any fishing Englishman!). The youngish wife of the hut owner (he himself, as she says, has left for Sacramento "on business") is Scottish by birth, ran away from her parents in early youth, and was brought here by fate. Her pretty features show clearly that she has seen something of life. She does the honors of the "house," cooks our meals with the help of an Indian lad as kitchen staff, and amuses me with the energetic manner in which she treats the Yankee and Swede (friends of her husband) who in his absence are trying to sweeten her life.

Forty to fifty steps from our hut is a camp where Indians spend the summer outside or in colorful, dirty tents, collecting wild raspberries which grow all over this valley (I must remind you that we are at a level of 4,000 feet!) and fishing for trout to provide to our gracious hostess and earn some money in return. The troupe is made up of about 20 people, counting men, women, and children. They seem to give no indications of hostility, so that the inhabitants of the block house, even without guests, have no reason to be afraid of them. Ernst and I went to visit them several times during the two days we spent there and observed the dismal life they lead, little different from animals. As the Swede told us, several of them were sick and were lying on the naked ground without any medication other than their squaws stroking them with healing hands. I observed this several times and undertook another kind of medication by bringing a bottle of wine that likely had better success. Such an Indian camp in the woods is highly picturesque, the glow of the fire like the one we saw at the salt lake, around which they cower, and the low wigwams. Their dogs are put all around as guards and growl when a stranger approaches. This warns the Indians and, when they are sure that the intruder has no bad intentions, they nimbly throw a rock or branch to the dogs from the fire and the dogs become calm and let you pass undisturbed. Consider our surroundings once more: is the company of two Germans, one Scottish woman, a Yankee, a Swede, and around 20 Indians not a strangely mixed and original company for such a faraway spot on earth?

There are other inhabitants in this valley and on the way here whose acquaintance we did not manage to make: rattlesnakes and gray bears—nice pets. The bears have retreated to the eastern part of the mountains, where they are hunted by the Indians and occasionally by the farmers from the plains; even the Swede and our guide have shot some, they say. The rattlesnakes have not been expelled from the area yet. Mr. Gordon killed one of these big things on his last trip and showed us the rattle. We ourselves found two dead snakes and saw the fresh traces of another one on our path. Adventures with them are a big part of the conversations among the people in the valley. The newest plan is to bring a few herds of pigs up here to kill them off. Pigs eat rattlesnakes and are not affected by their poison.

Clearly we did not sit still for the two days here. We took excursions in all directions even though the temperature was 26 degrees in the shade throughout and tempted us more than once to indulge in laziness. We visited a small lake called Mirror Lake, 45 feet deep, in which the mountains are reflected as in the Klönsee near Glarus. We saw two more wonderful falls, the Vernal and Nevada Falls. The Nevada is 700 feet high and can only be reached by strenuous climbing. All these are excursions that take six to eight hours with pretty long horseback rides on unfavorable terrain. The often lush and almost tropical vegetation of the valley is frequently replaced by rocky ground, where the stones are not big but rather slippery for four-legged creatures.

Despite everything, we called this our relaxing time, in contrast to the way back, the description of which I will allow myself to mention only briefly. We started with a ride of 36 miles, 14 hours on horseback on the first day, then on the second day, 12 miles on horseback and 41 in a vehicle. And on the third day we traveled 65 miles, at the end of which we had reached Stockton again. From there an 11-hour trip by steamship took us back at 1:00 in the morning.

This entire expedition would be a long trip for Europeans but it is an amusement party for natives here. Without counting the 125 miles from San Francisco to Stockton, we traveled 212 miles by cart and 140 miles by horse. Wasn't that hard riding in every sense of the word? This excursion was especially interesting for us quite apart from the spectacular landscape because a trip into the interior showed us the conditions and the inhabitants there, the generally dangerous conditions and the climate—in short, all the things worth knowing in detail. We are very satisfied and enjoy being done with it. But I can't help saying that except for the general experiences which are not even—at least according to the opinion of the inhabitants of San Francisco—an integral part of the excursion, the beauties of the valley may not be a sufficient equivalent for the cost in money, time, and strength. If we had turned back after the Big Trees we would have seen the most important part.

During our return trip and back here, we were received everywhere with great interest and people listened attentively to our realistic reports about what we had seen. I hope I am not wrong in believing that we, who were the first to contradict the general prejudice unhesitatingly, have managed to destroy the halo previously bestowed on this unknown area by earlier visitors, since it has even tempted ladies to come along and undertake the effort. Beyond Mariposa I saw a pretty young girl coming back from the valley in pitiable condition and heard her say: "Never again in my life; I am not made for bearing such hardships!" I would be glad if I was the cause for one or the other of them to think twice before facing such "hardships."

We will stay here for another four days and leave on Saturday, August 14 to ride the Pacific Railway all the way to Chicago, where we will stay for two days, then take a side trip to Canada and reach New York via Montreal, Lake George, Lake Champlain, and Saratoga. We will still have eight to ten days left for New York. To be honest, I had considered returning via the other side of the world, but unfortunately such a plan would take longer than Ernst's vacation allows, since we can't travel through Asia and would have to take the detour through India. My wish to visit China has just been awakened again by seeing the ship *Japan* arrive from Hong Kong in the harbor here. It is a spectacular ship, the biggest of the Pacific Mail Steamship Company, weighing 4,371 tons and able to transport 162 cabin and 1,288 steerage passengers. It manages the trip to Hong Kong (around 6,000 sea miles) in about 30 days. Let it all go!

I must return to the climate of San Francisco and its difference from the rest of California, which struck us again on our return. In Stockton it was 38 degrees in the sun; in San Francisco today we are almost cold in a summer coat, and the ladies on the steamship were wearing fur collars as we landed!

Occidental Hotel
San Francisco, August 14, 1869

This afternoon we are due to start heading east again! I can't help repeating how difficult the decision is not to travel back to you "the other way around." I would gladly renounce Canada and the projected stay in Paris if circumstances had allowed us to go through China!

We have been very active in the last days here: visiting a great number of factories (the workers being mainly Chinese), inspecting the storage areas of two important wine merchants and learning how Californian champagne is made, while trying all the kinds of Californian wine such as Port, Muscatel, Hock, Angelica—even brandy was not lacking; seeing and listening to the well-known popular speaker George Francis Train, Fenian* by birth, who declaimed in a public place to a dense crowd of dubious background (he railed about the now-burning Chinese question[68] and the relationship of the state of California to the federal government). In the evening, we visited various gambling dens and similar places which I don't want to describe further—we felt we must get to know this side of public life, to which one has easy access here anyway since it is all too evident—and finished our expeditions last night with another visit to a Chinese theater. We were lucky enough to witness a handsome "fight," the general thrashing about on stage that concludes every large section of a performance. All events on the Chinese stage last about as long as in reality, so that the same piece plays for several consecutive weeks; it was therefore indeed a fortuitous accident that we arrived in time for the fight. The racket around it was so terrible though that we hardly lasted a half hour in the theater.

And now adieu to California, adieu to the most interesting part of America we saw! And adieu to you lovely people! See you again in the States.

Tremont House[69]
Chicago, August 22, 1869

If I could speak at leisure instead of writing and were not being sidetracked continually by new impressions, I would give a great epilogue to the won-

---

* Supporter of an independent Irish republic.

derful country we are just leaving. I would make appropriate mention of the local curiosities—perfections and imperfections—the fertile, lush valleys and the uncultivated sandy deserts, the pretty farms and the areas destroyed by the miners, the ladies dressed in Parisian fashion and the Chinese, the Pacific Ocean, the Big Trees, Yosemite Valley. Where has this all gone now? In Europe, a trip of no more than 100 miles makes the impressions chase each other; "yesterday" is speedily superseded by "to-day." What should we say about the situation here, where we find ourselves taken by train for thousands of miles, without stops, to a completely new and very different environment, into another world? That is how different California is from the part of the States that was until recently called the "Far West."

After traveling on the great tracks for six days and five nights, we arrived here in the afternoon, the day before yesterday. Thanks to the admirable institution of the sleeping cars, we felt so well on arrival that, without exaggeration, we could have taken another trip as long again. Once the nerves are used to the continuous noise, which tends to be the case on the second day for everyone (not that there are any nervous Americans; they would only be fellow European travelers), nothing reminds us that we are on a train. As I described earlier, it is easy to believe that we are staying in an elegant hotel room. Sometimes we stand on the platform of the car looking at the view; sometimes we visit new acquaintances, sit down at a table to play at cards, go for a walk through the various cars to inspect the other travelers, read the latest newspapers from the East, of which a bundle was thrown over to us from the train passing the other way, etc.

On our entire trip there was only one small accident. On the second day, the train suddenly stopped in the middle of the desert. When we looked out the window we saw a train of several cars standing on the tracks in front of us, loaded with wood and in flames. As you know, there is only one track and so we had to wait till the fire was kind enough to go out, always afraid that the tracks would be damaged and our sojourn would be extended indefinitely. All kinds of things were tried to remove the burning stuff from the tracks. With the help of a number of Chinese who happened to be camping there to fix part of the train tracks, we all cooperated in moving a length of the tracks so that they would project beyond the embankment; we wanted to move the burning cars forward so that they would fall down the embankment. Once this difficult project was done we realized that the embers around the cars glowed so intensely that we could not approach close enough even with long sticks fastened to each other. So we decided for better or worse to watch the fire burn out and to refasten the tracks we had moved. After six hours, which were rather hard to bear in the middle of the day in the desert sun, everything was burned into black coal. We ran toward the wreckage eagerly to check the state of the tracks and noticed that they were not damaged, but the cross-ties were burned to ash. It took a while longer to remove unnecessary ties in other places and substitute them for the defective ones. Finally we could continue our trip. The funniest part of this event was that until we had caught up with the schedule, the eating houses did not have any food ready if we did not arrive at the correct time. So we had to go hungry, first for 11 hours—when we reached the place for supper which had been planning breakfast—and then fast another 14 hours. It was careless of us to have neglected bringing supplies as we had on the way there. We should have anticipated a case like this. However, several passengers who had brought supplies shared with the rest of us and a few pieces of buffalo tongue and antelope roast provided by our rescuers helped us out splendidly in this tight corner. To finish this episode, I want to praise once more my friends the Chinese, who proved their might yet again with the rather difficult work at the burning incident.

We were not as hot on the return trip, possibly because the Californian sun had dulled our senses or because it was not quite as hot as on the way there. In general we felt little affected by the temperature on this trip. There were fewer passengers in the sleeping car than last time, which also made the trip more pleasant. My chief companion was an old general who had been governor of Oregon[70] during the war and told us many stories, especially about repeated battles with the Indians there. He offered us letters of introduction to military institutes, but we declined because we would not have time enough to take advantage of them.

Once back in Omaha, the passengers of the Pacific Railway were transported across the Missouri by ferry: the train to Chicago is on the other side of the river. The transfer to the station on the other bank of the river was accomplished with four six-horse omnibuses in which we stayed during the ferry ride. This ferry clearly has a great capacity and it is reassuring not to doubt it when one sees the omnibuses, two heavy-laden four-horse baggage wagons and several two-horse carriages trotting onto it.

The State of Iowa, one of the best agricultural and farming states of the Union, begins beyond the Missouri. It can hardly be called densely populated, but the lush vegetation with pretty grass and whole forests of sunflowers are witness to the good soil which has already attracted many settlers who will soon increase in numbers. We reached Illinois beyond the Mississippi, which the train crossed on a bridge made of iron and wood. We bid a solemn and emotional good-bye to the river from this spot. This state is favored by nature, like Iowa, and culture has already progressed far; it culminates in its capital, Chicago,[71] the pride of Illinois, which ostentatiously calls itself the richest state and about which I will report various features to you.

Favorable chance gave us the opportunity to see the city in detail and "with commentary." For when we visited our banker (which we did immediately on arrival, hoping to find letters from you) the gentleman volunteered to show us around in his carriage the next morning and to lead us around the sights of this city. As he says, it is his ambition to show Chicago to Europeans from its best side and for this reason he wanted to be our cicerone. We took this tour yesterday morning. It lasted more than seven hours and served its purpose so well that we do not find it necessary to stay longer and are continuing our trip this afternoon.

The life story of our banker is interesting enough that I will mention it briefly in my report. It is indicative of certain American conditions.[72] Our friend is now 45 years old, born in Westphalia. He studied theology in Bonn and, before he finished his studies, was convinced by an American pastor, whom he met at the university, to become a pastor in America. For ten years he was a preacher. At the start of his tenure, solely to announce his presence, he wrote a pamphlet in which he advocated abolition of the Bible as a teaching tool in the public schools. This pamphlet created much attention. The more the orthodox despised him, the more the opposite party supported him. Finally he was tired of the constant religious arguments back and forth, which he felt obliged to address all the time. He quickly decided to become a lawyer. Now, when the rebellion in the South started he immediately left his new profession and dedicated himself to political battle as a raging abolitionist. The radicals approved of his activities; he became a state senator for four years, then lieutenant governor of Illinois for as long. He administered both of those positions during the most difficult times and now, all of a sudden, he is a prosperous banker even though, as he says himself, he knows nothing about this business!

What he told of his deeds as lieutenant governor amused us no end, especially when he had to pass the troops of his state in review, even though he hardly knew the difference between the uniforms of an infantryman and a cavalryman; how he had to promote officers to colonel without having any idea of the capabilities of the individual, or how strangely he was affected when he was able to exercise his right to pardon a man sentenced to death. The present President Grant was his secretary while he was governor, and he recalls that he would often throw a letter to him (the President) saying: Please copy this! I hardly need to tell you that such a person was just what we needed. We questioned him in all directions, discussed political and financial issues, and were instructed by him in great detail about everything we wanted to know.

In addition we also saw Chicago. It has grown to such importance that people other than its inhabitants must recognize this if they want to be impartial. In 1840, the city had 3,500 inhabitants; now it has more than 300,000. The location of the city is very favorable and its position as the chief commercial city of the West seems assured, despite the rivalry with St. Louis. It has actually overtaken the latter already. Thirteen train routes lead here; Lake Michigan and the Erie Canal provide waterway connections directly to New York and even to the ocean.

Trading in grains is Chicago's main business; last year 65 million bushels of grain were exported. We were very taken by a visit to the so-called elevators, buildings in which the loose grain is hauled up by machines as it arrives on train cars (hence the name) and poured into the ships waiting on the other side; within a half hour these machines empty about 20 carloads or more.

The equipment to provide drinking water for the city is also very impressive. A tunnel with an eight-foot diameter runs about two miles under the lake toward its middle; from the end of the tunnel, a 100-foot-high pipe extends a little above the surface of the lake. In this pipe there are valves at several places which can let in water from various depths. At the shore, the water from the tunnel is pumped into enormous reservoirs by three machines of 1,600 horsepower each, and from there the city receives its water. The reason for bringing it from so far is that movement near the shore clouds the water; a little way from the shore it is so clear that it can be consumed unfiltered.

Among the most peculiar things here is the widely occurring removal of houses, which is practiced on a grand scale. Big houses made of stone wander around in this way. During the process, the people stay living in them and lead their lives as usual. One street for instance, which is about as long as Behrensstrasse and consists entirely of stone buildings, was moved back by 25 feet to make the area more beautiful; the huge hotel in which we are staying was only recently moved up by seven feet. The following announcement in today's paper will not surprise you after this: "The long wooden house to the West of C. W. Burt's brick building in Farnam Street, belonging to John McCreary Esq. is being moved to the corner of California and Seventeenth Streets." This is a friendly announcement in which Mr. McCreary lets his acquaintances know of his change of address. If someone in Europe who is not familiar with the conditions here saw this paper by chance, he would not know what to make of the word "moved."

Chicago in general makes a bigger and more complete impression than any other city on this continent, with the exception of New York, Boston, and Philadelphia. Even San Francisco cannot compete with the size of the houses, the width and liveliness of the streets, and the beauty of the stores. It would not take much clairvoyance to expect a great future for Chicago.

This afternoon we are starting a 24-hour train trip to Canada, first to Toronto, and from there the next day by ship to Montreal via the rapids of the St. Lawrence River, which we are anticipating with great eagerness.

St. Lawrence Hall[73]
Montreal (Canada), August 26, 1869

We left Chicago this time in something called a hotel car, a kind of train compartment we had not seen before; besides sleeping accommodations, lavatory, etc. which are part of the sleeping cars, we were also served our meals there so that we did not have to leave the train at all during the entire trip if we did not want to. I understand that they are starting to use such cars on the trip from New York to San Francisco; they are even used on some of the eastern routes of two- to three-day trips. They are the height of comfort. A supervising black appears three times a day at the usual meal times with a printed menu and, after receiving our order, makes three Negroes set up a small, nicely appointed table in front of us, on which we are served the meal. The food is quite good (it is cooked on the premises). The only problem with these hotel cars is that one can smell the food being prepared before it is served. When several people eat at the same time the car with its small tables looks just like a restaurant.

Since the trip had few remarkable things to reveal, we devoted ourselves to studying this picture and eating our supper, for which it was time soon after our departure from Chicago, and went to bed rather early. About two hours beyond Chicago, we crossed the border to Canada; at the moment we are again enjoying the patronage of Queen Victoria and are breathing monarchic air; very soothing for the royalist in me!

We looked around Hamilton, a friendly little city of 25,000 inhabitants on the shores of Lake Ontario, spent a day in Toronto (which contains a beautifully planned university and museum in which, to my delight, I espied the following printed message in the corners: "The dirty practice of spitting is not allowed in these buildings." This remark was aimed at the visitors from the States). Tomorrow we will proceed past Lake George, according to plan, on our way to New York.

The trip across the Rapids of St. Lawrence is remarkable and equals the most impressive sights of America. The rapids recur at many point with drops of varying heights from Prescott—the place where the St. Lawrence flows out of Lake Ontario—to Montreal. The longest and strongest are the Lachine Rapids, eight miles above Montreal. Because of these rapids, the magnificent river that is as wide as the Elbe at Cuxhafen is only navigable for sailboats from Montreal on. No other boats except a particular kind of steamship can pass them. An Indian pilot comes on board when one gets close and takes over the steering of the ship; then it takes four men to hold the tiller. Three others are ready at a second tiller should something happen to the first. The first moments create a strange feeling when one is pushed along with astounding speed by the falling waters and through the whirlpools of the excited element. Once we shot past the half-destroyed rump of a steamship which had been guided by ignorant hands and was stranded at one of the frequent rocky formations in the rapids. All its passengers drowned since there was no way to get close enough to save them.

The trip on Lake Ontario lasted 20 hours; the one on the St. Lawrence River, eight hours. The latter was partly rich in picturesque views, especially where we passed the Thousand Islands (an extensive group of small, rocky, and scenic wooded islands). On arriving in Montreal, we immediately noticed the huge two-mile-long railroad bridge, Victoria Bridge, across the St. Lawrence. It is constructed with a tubular system supported by 23 pillars, 242 feet apart, except for the middle ones which are as much as 330 feet apart. I believe it really is the longest in the world, as the Americans say.

The city of 150,000 inhabitants is half French, half English and unusual in that these contrasts are very noticeable. It is otherwise not very attractive. We saw some of the public buildings which had been recommended: the Medical College, Notre Dame Cathedral, and the Court House among others, without finding them very remarkable. The Quay is pretty with its many big ships, among them the passenger steamships going to Quebec, similar to the ones used between Newport and New York.

The dialect of the Montreal population is unfortunately impossible to understand. The French keep wanting to speak English, the English French; the French names are pronounced in English, the English ones in French. Nobody can make heads or tails of it!

5th Avenue Hotel
New York, August 31, 1869

What do you say to our having arrived here again? Are you as comfortable as we, who see New York and Berlin almost as neighboring cities? I think there is no better proof for the endlessness of the American continent. The immense distances we crossed as if flying, the hundreds of miles of country cultivated sparsely or not at all, have given way to a metropolis—such memories make us believe that we have almost arrived in Europe again or at least are not separated further by the Atlantic Ocean than the Channel separates England from the shores of the Continent.

After we left the Hudson steamship yesterday morning, in which we had traveled from Albany and where we had slept comfortably in a stateroom, we sat at the window of our room and looked down on Broadway and its unchanged and so-familiar life. We both felt and admitted to each other that we were as glad as in our happiest moments so far. First I must thank our kind fate that we both enjoyed this beautiful time without any disturbing illness or other disadvantages. If I could give you this message instantly I am sure you would join in our thanks. Then I read the letter from you in which I found only good news and gave August 30 a big red mark, even if not in the calendar (since I did not have it handy) but in my mind.

Your letters are from July 26 and I realize reading them that you did not even know definitively that we had gone to California and were worried about that to a certain extent. How glad I am to report that we not only completed this trip, but that it was so beautiful and interesting and that it went as well as it possibly could. My only regret is that this message will only reach you in 14 days at the earliest! The contrast between the past (your letters) and the present (my state of mind) is so great that I was tempted to send a telegraphic message to speed up the further contrast between now and the future (the arrival of this letter).

I hope that these lines will reach you in time so that you will be able to follow us when we are swimming on the ocean again; we are planning to leave on September 14 with the *Holsatia* out of Hamburg. The two weeks till then we will spend in New York, maybe taking an occasional excursion to watering places like Newport or Long Branch.

We visited the local Baden-Baden, called Saratoga, the day before yesterday; it is supposed to outdo all the rest of the spas by far. Sometimes I think that in this part of the world everything is either exaggerated or understated in comparison to our European understanding and usage. Saratoga is exaggerated. I know no spa such as Saratoga in such an unimportant place, with no promenades, with such mineral springs, colossal hotels, exorbitant dress (and prices), with such crowds of people, and with such a show of dullness and tastelessness, with such endless boredom. Naturally I refer to the boredom of people being there for a longer time; if one stays, as we did, for 24 hours there is enough to see that this does not happen. Anything longer than 24 hours must be horrible. Compared to hotels in Saratoga, the Swiss ones are mere doll houses. There were 800 people in ours; others were just as full. I can't tell you exactly the number of Negroes serving in the dining hall; 60 is likely too little rather than too much.

I will write nothing of the senseless overdressing that we see at luncheon, in the drawing rooms, and on the covered promenades in the hotel courtyard, where there is usually music after meals (and what music!). I am ignorant of the technical terms to give you an impression of what unfolds here. Especially in the evening at the dance "reunions" in the big drawing room, everything is let loose, especially the hair, and ball gowns appear which would be put on exhibit like a princess's dowry at home. The jewelry is in the right proportion to all that. It is not surprising, watching the dress, that the fashionable ladies here rarely travel with fewer than four suitcases. To give you a sense of the luggage arriving and leaving our hotel in Saratoga, I will tell you that together with us, 24 large suitcases (the well-known American wooden three-level kind) arrived from the train station, and the porter told me that there are as many again to be picked up from there. This is all from one train to one hotel. As our friend told us, we are witnessing Saratoga in the brilliance of high season. A few hours after us, President Grant arrived and was received by great crowds and a deputation. We avoided a meeting with his American Majesty this time because we had no time to lose.

Another fashionable place like Saratoga is the Fort William Henry Hotel near Caldwell on Lake George. This hotel is a kind of Beau Rivage, isolated also but three times as big. In dress and dance it resembled Saratoga, but the society seemed more purely republican aristocracy. I get the impression that the demimonde stays away from pretty views, of which Lake George has many to offer, even though American reports exaggerate its beauty: "Unequalled (!) even by the famous Lake of Como of Switzerland," says a printed description of the lake, for which the editor would deserve reproach had we not been used to "in the world" by now. I am quite glad that we have seen this side of American life as well. Does a society where the young people run around with ribbons in their buttonholes which are supposed to look like medals really have the flavor of a great republic?

5ᵗʰ Avenue Hotel
New York, September 10, 1869

If all goes well you will receive this letter, the last one "from America," only one or two days before the telegram announcing our arrival in Cherbourg. Our crossing looks as excellent as we could hope for. Yesterday afternoon, A. invited us to a dinner which the captain of the *Holsatia*, by the name of Ehlers, gave on board and to which he had invited about 20 gentlemen. It was very comfortable, guaranteed by a host like "fat old Ehlers" (as the captain is called by a friend) who knows how to live richly at sea. I like the old gentleman quite well; his slightly rough and strong, but always good-natured manners are like those frequently attributed to captains in novels. He made merciless sport of Ernst when he asked whether the equinoctial storms would not be hard to deal with. The captain laughed and kept referring all evening to Mr. "Wessfahl's" (as he called him in his Hamburg dialect) equinoctial storms. The first officer, who also dined with us, seems a pleasant person, and the physician on board is an old acquaintance of mine from Berlin; again a strange coincidence!

After dinner we went on deck, where sailors in dress uniforms attended to us; we smoked and looked at the stars (without deep, nostalgic contemplation) and only left the ship at 12, to return to New York by way of the bay. The Hamburg ships anchor at Jersey City, that is, off the mainland.

Today, in the company of one of our acquaintances, we toured several public educational institutions for blacks and whites and listened to the teaching; I must admit we did not pay the necessary attention in the case of some girls' schools in which the students were already grown up and included in their number several typical American beauties. Later we toured the treasury of the United States in the Treasury Building. There we were introduced to General Butterfield, the head of the department, and obtained entry which, as I was told, is rarely granted.

Now I have to close since the letter is supposed to be transported by the Inman Steamer leaving in a few hours—the only passenger ship which will arrive in Europe before us.

Grand Hotel
Paris, September 29, 1869
We left New York in beautiful weather. Everything in the first two days went as desired. The company was pleasant, even if only two young girls were present (one of whom, alas, was engaged and could hardly be counted): we played, made conversation, and vegetated in a tolerable way. On the third day the wind suddenly turned and came so directly from the East that within 24 hours we lost about eight hours of the usual time scheduled for these crossings. Captain and passengers made long faces;

the latter were forced to stay below because of the rain, and their mood was rather dampened. One day later, three gentlemen from first class complained of sore throats and not being able to swallow; a medical examination resulted in a diagnosis of diphtheria. Soon the doctor had it also, then another seven passengers and four stewards, and finally your son also. I became a patient on the sixth day, and unfortunately one of the worst off. Those who have never experienced life on a ship do not know what it is like to be sick on board. For the rest of the trip I had nothing but a cup of broth a day and could not sleep for a minute. A strong and constant wind from the southwest produced such high waves from the side that the ship rolled fiercely enough to make lying down impossible. Even our captain, the old salt, could not close his eyes for 24 hours during the worst time. I spent one night on the couch in the drawing room, another on that of our cabin or on the floor, on chairs, in other words in various positions. The movement of the ship caused the lunch plates to fly from one side of the table to the other and not a bottle could stay upright; they nailed boards on the open side of the beds so people would not be hurled out of them.

To make a good ending, our old friend fog enveloped us again one and a half days before we arrived at Plymouth. The foghorn blew every minute and we had to proceed very slowly because of the nearness to the Channel. It was a depressing situation. In the middle of the next night, the engines suddenly stopped; we were close to the Scilly Islands (west of England) and would have run aground if the fog had not opened up for a moment and the captain, who had been on the bridge all night, had not stopped the ship with a jolt. On the next day around noon, Ehlers thought we were close to Plymouth; therefore he let the ship lie still and waited for the fog to lift. We could not see a hand in front of our eyes and no observations had been tracked for the last day and a half. We might as well have been on the moon.

We stayed in the same spot for three hours, the foghorn blowing constantly; when we gathered at noon no one spoke a word. Suddenly the steward came in saying: "It has cleared up!" Of course everyone was on deck in one jump and we saw my old acquaintance, the Eddystone light, in front of us, just as if ordered. Now we sailed full steam ahead and reached Plymouth in four hours, left again in the evening at 8:30, and greeted the harbor of Cherbourg the next morning at 6:30 with a gun salute and a stout-hearted Hurray for the Old Country!

NOTES

1. The *Scotia* was a steamship of the Cunard Line, the British transatlantic shipping company, built in 1862 and sunk in 1904.

2. Probably Captain C. H. Judkins.

3. When Charles Dickens undertook a trip through the United States with his wife in 1842, he thought it was a joke when he found "this terrible hole of a place" on the *Britannia*, having been promised a salon. See Charles Dickens, *American Notes* (London: Chapman and Hall, 1842).

4. Around 6 degrees Celsius. The Reaumur temperature scale was widely used in Germany and France during the nineteenth century but lost its importance with the official conversion to the Celsius scale in 1901. One degree Reaumur equals 1.25 degrees Celsius.

5. Probably Hermann Althoff.

6. This expression is based on the Danish author Ludvig Holber's drama *The Political Tinker* (which premiered in 1722 in Copenhagen) and alludes to empty and silly gossip about politics.

7. Likely Wheeler H. Bristol.

8. The Epsom Derby, in existence since 1779, is the most prestigious British horse race.

9. The musician Patrick Gilmore organized the National Peace Jubilee as a onetime event in Boston in 1869.

10. Felix Mendelssohn Bartholdy.

11. See note 5.

12. Parker House in Boston, Massachusetts, was established by Harvey D. Parker and is the oldest and most noble of the city's hotels. It was the meeting place of the Boston Saturday Club, founded in 1855. Literary giants like Ralph Waldo Emerson, Henry Wadsworth Longfellow, Henry David Thoreau, and Nathaniel Hawthorne congregated there. John F. Kennedy announced his candidacy for Congress in the press hall of this hotel. In addition, the place is famous for the Parker House roll and the Boston cream pie, the recipes for which go back to the nineteenth century.

13. Baring Brothers and Co. was an investment bank in London.

14. See note 9.

15. The music for the opera *Der Freischütz* was composed by Carl Maria von Weber in the Romantic style. The opera premiered at the Royal Theater in Berlin in 1821.

16. The concerts of the Liebig'sche band were led by Karl Liebig (1808–1872), the oboist and director of the music corps of the Prussian Alexander Regiment. From 1843 onward, they presented orchestral concerts, playing overtures and symphonies at various places in Berlin.

17. The Exchange Hotel in Richmond, Virginia, was designed by Isaiah Rogers in the Neoclassical style and opened in 1841. It was called "The Lion of the Day" because of its gigantic dimensions and its multifunctional concept. It housed the hotel, post office, reading rooms, baths, and businesses.

18. In the summer of 1868, Ernst Mendelssohn-Bartholdy traveled through Scotland.

19. Alexander Mendelssohn lived in the house at Jägerstraße 52.

20. The Battle of Bunker Hill was fought at the beginning of the War of American Independence on June 17, 1775, ending with a dearly won victory for the British.

21. The Longfellow House in Cambridge, Massachusetts, served George Washington as the first headquarters for the Continental Army.

22. Ernst Mendelssohn-Bartholdy's parents owned a summer place in Charlottenburg near Berlin, Lützowstrasse 2.

23. Ernst Mendelssohn-Bartholdy is referring here to the Hermann Gerson department store, founded in 1838 in Berlin and well known for its innovative ladies' apparel (*Maison de Nouveautés*). In 1869, it became the purveyor for the royal houses of Prussia, Berlin, Sweden, and Norway.

24. The Hermann Gerson department store was at Werderscher Markt 5.

25. Likely Karl Mendelssohn Bartholdy.

26. Around 34°C or 92°F.

27. Edward Virginius Valentine.

28. Henry Horatio Wells.

29. Henry Horatio Wells.

30. Ernst Westphal.

31. Around 44°C and 38°C, respectively, or 100°F.

32. Henry Horatio Wells.

33. Probably Elizabeth Valentine, born Mosby.

34. The Continental in Philadelphia, Pennsylvania, was one of the noblest hotels in the United States. Built in the Italian style and opened in 1860, it boasted an elevator and could accommodate 1,000 guests in 700 rooms. On February 21, 1861, Abraham Lincoln learned in this hotel from Allan Pinkerton and Frederick W. Seward of an assassination attempt planned in Baltimore.

35. See note 34.

36. Probably Mann S. Valentine Jr.

37. Probably Hugo von Krause.

38. Probably Hugo von Krause.

39. Likely Frederick Tracy Dent.

40. The Cataract House in Niagara Falls, New York, was built as a three-story log cabin by David Chapman in 1825. It originally belonged to Judge Samuel DeVeaux and was situated on the banks of the river. Reconstructed by various owners, it was the largest hotel in town. It burned to the ground on October 14, 1945.

41. Probably Rudolf Schelske.

42. Alexander Mendelssohn.

43. Probably Hugo Oppenheim.

44. Robert Barth.

45. Obviously freely citing "The Canticle of the Sun" by Francis of Assisi.

46. Probably Isaak F. Willcox and his wife, Mary Bell, née Caster, who were married on March 18, 1869, in Henderson County.

47. Paul Mendelssohn-Bartholdy.

48. Sebastian Hensel.

49. Wilhelm Hensel.

50. The Von der Heydts were a banking family in Elberfeld.

51. Charles Blondin first crossed Niagara Falls on a tightrope 1100 feet long, 160 feet above the water, on June 30, 1859.

52. Girard College was opened in 1848 and exists to this day.

53. The largest temple in Paestum, in the Campania region of Italy, goes back to 540 AD and is dedicated to the goddess Hera.

54. The palacelike Southern Hotel in St. Louis, Missouri, was built in the Italian style in 1866 between Furth and Walnut Streets. It had six stories and 350 rooms and was favored by Mark Twain for its excellent billiard tables. In 1877 it burned to the ground; it was reopened in 1881 and finally closed in 1912 and torn down in 1933.

55. The German-language newspaper *Westliche Post* appeared in St. Louis from 1857 to 1938. John Pulitzer was one of the team of editors from 1868 to 1873.

56. The newspaper editor Conrad Bolz was a character in the drama *The Journalists* by Gustav Freytag.

57. Galt House, owned by W. C. Galt at the beginning of the nineteenth century, was renowned as the most noble hotel in Louisville. In 1865 it was destroyed by fire and reopened as an expensive and pompous structure with a big ballroom. Prominent guests were Stephen Douglass, Edwin Booth, Charles Dickens, P. T. Barnum, Tom Thumb, and US presidents Zachary Taylor, James Buchanan, Abraham Lincoln, Ulysses S. Grant, and Rutherford B. Hayes as well as Jefferson Davis, the president of the Confederate States of America. In 1864 the generals of the Union, Ulysses S. Grant and William T. Sherman, planned their military strategies in Galt House.

58. Robert Barth.

59. The Metropolitan Hotel in Omaha, Nebraska, was one of a number of hotels that sprang up in this fast-growing city after 1863. The choice of this hotel was a last resort. "It was so full here that we could not get a room in the hotel we had planned to live in." We can only speculate which hotel was meant in the original plan; most likely it would have been the Grand Central Hotel.

60. Townsend House in Salt Lake City, built in 1869, was one of the first addresses in the city in 1869 and was torn down at the end of the nineteenth century.

61. Marcel Jozon.

62. Eddystone Light is a lighthouse fourteen kilometers off the shore of Cornwall on the English coast.

63. St. Stephen was one of the first Christian martyrs; St. Leocardia was a Christian martyr of the fourth century. The reason for the allusion is unclear.

64. The Occidental Hotel of San Francisco, California, was built in the Italian style between 1861 and 1869 by the architects C. Hyatt, Th. Johnston, and W. Mooser. It was on

Montgomery Street between Sutter and Bush Streets. It was one of the three biggest and noblest hotels of the city and was destroyed in the big earthquake of 1906.

65. Alexis de Tocqueville, *De la démocratie en Amérique* (Brussels: Hauman/Société Belge de Librairies, 1835/1840).

66. Clark's Station was named after Galen Clark.

67. According to legend, the archbishop of Mainz, Hatto I or Hatto II (ninth–tenth century), was eaten up by mice as punishment for his hard-heartedness toward the starving population.

68. The Burlingame Treaty of 1868 was a contract of friendship between the United States and China. It favored Chinese emigration into the United States and eliminated the labor shortage on the West Coast. After the Chinese workers participated in the completion of the transcontinental railway, they became a threat of competition on the labor market for the other immigrants, which resulted in anti-Chinese resentment. In the 1870s, there was open hostility in Californian cities, leading to the Chinese Exclusion Act of 1882, which prevented further Chinese immigration for decades. See Charles J. McClain, *In Search of Equality: The Chinese Struggle against Discrimination in Nineteenth-Century America* (Berkeley: University of California Press, 1994).

69. Tremont House, in Chicago, Illinois, was the successor to the first Chicago Tremont House, built in the Neoclassical style in 1850. During the time of extensive house moving in Chicago in the middle of the nineteenth century, it was the largest building of the city and housed, among others, the central office of the Republican Party during the National Convention. The building was destroyed in 1871 during the great Chicago fire.

70. Addison C. Gibbs.

71. At the time of this writing, the capital of Illinois had been moved from its original location in Kaskaskia to Vandalia and thence to Springfield. Chicago was certainly the chief city of Illinois.

72. Franz Arnold Hoffmann.

73. The Saint Lawrence Hall Hotel in Montreal, Canada, was opened in 1851. The address was Great Saint James Street 13. It was regarded as the leading hotel of the city. For a time, it served as the central office of the Grand Trunk Railway, the leading Canadian railway system. Prominent guests included the Prince of Wales, Charles Dickens, and George Brown.

LIST OF NAMES

The following is a list of the people alluded to in the travel letters who could be identified.

Althoff, Hermann (1835–1877). Ophthalmologist and surgeon; went to the United States in 1845, returned to Germany for his medical degree, and received his doctorate in Berlin in 1858. He went back and forth between Germany and the United States several times, was among the founders of the New York Ophthalmological Society, and was elected twice as its chairman. Pages 25, 27, 103.

Barth, Robert (1815). Born and raised in Prussia; he moved to St. Louis in 1839 and was partner in the bank Angelrodt & Barth, director of railroads, director of the Perpetual Insurance Company (after 1843) and of the Phoenix Floating Dock Company, and president of the German Savings Association. Consul of Prussia; after 1868, of the North German Federation; after 1871, of the German Reich. Pages 48, 59.

Bates, Joshua (1788–1864). After 1828, senior partner of Baring Brothers & Co. Page 30.

Bristol, Wheeler H. (1818–1904). Engineer and Democratic politician; treasurer of the State of New York, 1868–1871. He was confirmed in his duties in the election of 1869 but conceded to his Republican opponent in 1871. Pages 25, 45, 59.

Butterfield, Daniel (1831–1901). Businessman, general in the Union Army during the Civil War, and assistant treasurer of the United States after 1869. He was connected to a bribery scandal that resulted in the collapse of the gold price on September 24 (Black Friday), 1869, and induced him to resign his job. Page 104.

Clark, Galen (1814–1910). Owner of a small hotel and guide through Yosemite Valley who also wrote books such as *The Big Trees of California* (1907), *Indians of the Yosemite Valley and Vicinity* (1904), and *The Yosemite Valley* (1910). Pages 88–89.

Cole, Nathan (1825–1904). Republican and mayor of St. Louis from April 13, 1869, to 1871. Page 75.

Coulter, George W. Founded Maxwell's Creek in 1853, a settlement in the middle of California, which was officially renamed Coulterville in 1872. Page 86.

Davis, Jefferson (1808–1889). President of the secessionist Confederate States of America 1861–1865. Page 40.

Dent, Frederick Tracy (1820–1892). Brigadier general and brother-in-law of President Ulysses S. Grant. Page 45.

Dickens, Charles (1812–1870). English writer; traveled through the United States in 1842. Page 15.

Ehlers, H. Captain of the *Holsatia* after it began sailing on March 9, 1868, from 1868 to 1870. Pages 104–105.

Gerolt, Freiherr Friedrich Joseph Karl von (1797–1879). Royal Prussian privy councilor and special envoy to the United States. Page 42.

Gibbs, Addison C. (1925–1886). Governor of Oregon. However, he was no general. Page 92.

Gordon, Peter (1830–1903). Mountain man. Page 87.

Grant, Ulysses S. (1822–1885). Commander-in-chief of the Union Army during the Civil War, 1864–1865; US president, 1869–1877. Pages 26, 28, 31–34, 41, 45–46, 48, 98, 103.

Harlan, James (1820–1899). US Secretary of the Interior, 1865–1866; senator from Iowa, 1867–1873. Page 75.

Hensel, Sebastian (1830–1890). Farmer and entrepreneur; cousin of Ernst Mendelssohn-Bartholdy. Page 51.

Hensel, Wilhelm (1794–1861). Painter; uncle of Ernst Mendelssohn-Bartholdy. Page 51.

Hoffmann, Franz (Francis) Arnold (1822–1903). Born in the Prussian province of Westphalia, he emigrated to the United States in 1840, where he was a teacher, pastor, and writer. After 1851 he studied law in Chicago and became a lawyer. He switched from the Democratic Party to the Republican Party on the question of slavery. Lieutenant governor of Illinois, 1861–1865. After the Civil War he founded the International Bank. In 1875 he retired to his country seat in Jefferson, Wisconsin, and concentrated on agriculture and plant cultivation. Pages 97ff.

Hooper, William Henry (1813–1882). Was one of the Mormons settling Utah in 1850. He was a representative of the Utah territories in Congress, 1865–1873. Pages 56, 69–74.

Huster, A. Royal Court Caterer in Berlin. Page 72.

Jeffries, Benjamin Joy (1833–1915). Ophthalmologist in Boston who researched color blindness and used employees of the railways for a study he initiated in the 1880s. Pages 27, 32.

Jozon, Marcel (1830–1918). French engineer. Page 62.

Judkins, C. H. Ship's captain. Page 14.

Krause, Hugo von (died 1874). Prussian/German diplomat, legation secretary, and later ambassador to London. Pages 42, 45–46, 48.

Lee, Robert E. (1807–1870). Commander-in-chief of the North Virginia army of the secessionist Confederate States of America during the Civil War, 1861–1865. Page 46.

Levy, Jules (1838–1903). Born in England, started his soloist carrier in the United States, and was hired by Theodore Thomas for summer concerts in Central Park. Levy called himself the "world's greatest cornetist." Page 31.

Lingaard, William (1839–1927). English comedian and singer who settled in New York and, at the time, had the reputation of being hilariously funny. Page 34.

Mendelssohn, Alexander (1798–1871). Senior partner of the private bank Mendelssohn & Co. Pages 33, 47.

Mendelssohn Bartholdy, Felix (1809–1847). Composer; uncle to Ernst Mendelssohn-Bartholdy. Pages 27, 30, 41, 69, 87.

Mendelssohn Bartholdy, Karl (1838–1897). Historian, son of Felix Mendelssohn Bartholdy, and cousin to Ernst Mendelssohn-Bartholdy. Pages 35, 37.

Mendelssohn-Bartholdy, Paul (1812–1874). Banker, father of Ernst Mendelssohn-Bartholdy, and brother of Felix Mendelssohn Bartholdy. Page 51.

Oppenheim, Hugo (1847–1921). Banker and grandson of Alexander Mendelssohn; lived in London in 1868–1869, where he is likely to have had regular contact with Ernst Mendelssohn-Bartholdy. Page 47.

Parepa-Rosa, Euphrosyne, born Parepa (1836–1874). British soprano who stayed in the United States after a tour in 1867 and promoted operatic arias in the provinces. Page 31.

Peabody, George (1795–1869). London entrepreneur who was called the "father of philanthropy." Pages 14–15.

Ryerson, Beekman van Buren (1809–1881). Inventor of the diving bell and a centrifugal mill used to extract gold. Page 86.

Schelske, Rudolf (1830–1906). Ophthalmologist who married Ernst Mendelssohn-Bartholdy's sister Katherine (1846–1906) in 1868. Page 47.

Schlaginweit, Robert (von) (1833–1906). Traveled the United States from New York to San Francisco in 1869 and 1880 and published, among others, *Die pacifischen Eisenbahnen in Nordamerika* [The Pacific Railroads in North America] (1886), *Die Mormonen oder die Heiligen vom jüngsten Tage. Von der Entstehung bis zur Gegenwart* [The Mormons or Latter-Day Saints. From Their Origins to the Present] (1874), and *Die Prärien des amerikanischen Westens* [The Prairies of the American West] (1876). Page 90.

Schurz, Karl (1829–1906). Activist in the March Revolution of 1848 who served in the Baden Revolutionary Army in 1849 and fled in the same year from Rastatt to France. In 1850, he made a secret trip to Berlin and participated in freeing Gottfried Kinkel from Spandau prison. Emigrated to the United States, 1852; leading politician of the Republicans; after 1867, co-owner and editor of the *Westliche Post* in St. Louis; senator from Missouri, 1869–1875. Page 56.

Sumner, Charles (1811–1874). American politician, bitter opponent of slavery; initially a supporter of Ulysses S. Grant, later his opponent because of numerous corruption scandals. Page 48.

Thomas, Theodore (1835–1905). Violinist and conductor; born in Esens, East Friesia; emigrated to the United States in 1848; after 1864, organized summer concerts with his own orchestra, among other places in Central Park. He was also director of the New York Philharmonic and first director of the Chicago Symphony Orchestra and helped Richard Wagner rise to popularity in the United States. Page 31.

Tiffany, Otis Henry (1825–1891). Methodist preacher and activist of the American Party (the Know Nothing movement) in Pennsylvania, whose goals included restrictive immigration and anti-Catholic policies. Page 75.

Train, George Francis (1829–1904). Eccentric businessman, writer, and world traveler. Page 94.

Valentine, Edward Virginius (1838–1930). Sculptor; studied in Paris and Italy as well as with the sculptor August Kiss (1802–1865) in Berlin in the years before 1865. Pages 38, 41–42.

Valentine, Elizabeth, born Mosby (1801–1872). Pages 41–42.

Valentine, Mann S., Junior (1824–1892). Founder of the Valentine Museum in Richmond. Page 42.

Wells, Henry Horatio (1823–1890). Lawyer, member of the Republican party, and governor of Virginia, 1868–1869. Page 38.

Westphal, Ernst (1834–1903). Lawyer and director of railroads; cousin to Ernst Mendelssohn-Bartholdy. Pages 14, 16ff.

Young, Brigham (1801–1877). Since 1830, member of the Mormons; became president of the religious community in 1844 after the violent death of its founder, Joseph Smith Jr., and was regarded as its "second prophet" ever since. Pages 66–67, 69–74.

BARBARA HAIMBERGER THIEM

is a performing cellist and teaches at Colorado State University.
She spends the summers in Austria and Germany, keeping up the
tradition of gathering at Traunsee in the old family place,
surrounded by immediate and more distant family members.

GERTRUD GRAUBART CHAMPE, PhD

is a professional translator with an interest in
European cultural history.

Lightning Source UK Ltd.
Milton Keynes UK
UKOW04n2013161017

311090UK00003B/23/P